Grade 3

Wonders
CALIFORNIA Content Reader

B

The McGraw·Hill Companies

 Macmillan/McGraw-Hill

Published by Macmillan/McGraw-Hill, of McGraw-Hill Education, a division of The McGraw-Hill Companies, Inc., Two Penn Plaza, New York, New York 10121.

Printed in the United States of America

   7 8 9 10 WEB 14 13 12 11

Contents

Contents

Energy All Around

Did you know that whenever work is done, energy (EN•uhr•jee) is involved?

Light from the Sun is the main source of energy for Earth. Plants use light to make food and grow. When animals eat plants, some of that energy is transferred to them.

Energy can be stored in food, batteries, and fuel. **Fuel** (FYEWL) is a substance such as gasoline, coal, or wood that we burn for energy. Machines use this type of stored energy to heat buildings. Machines can also change stored energy into moving energy to run most cars, planes, and trains. Our bodies use the stored energy in food to move, grow, and stay warm. When you run, you heat up. You convert the stored energy of the food you have eaten into motion and heat.

All moving objects have energy that can be carried to other objects. The energy of your moving arm is carried to the bowling ball when you throw it. The energy of that ball transfers to the pins it hits.

Energy can be carried from one place to another by waves. Waves are disturbances that move through matter or space. They include sound waves, light waves, and ocean waves. The energy that moves an ocean wave up and down is transferred to any objects in the water. Sound waves push air around and carry energy from one place to another.

Electrical energy is carried in a current from power plants, through wires, to electrical sockets. When a plug is put into a socket, electrical energy moves through the cord and changes to the energy that lights lamps and turns on television sets and computers.

▲ **A bowler uses energy to knock down pins.**

The Future of Energy

One day, more and more of our power will come from the Sun, the wind, the ocean, and even plants!

Sun Power

Russell Illig/Photodisc/Getty Images

To collect sunlight, people put special panels on the roofs of buildings. The special panels take in sunlight. The panels turn the sunlight into electricity. The electricity can be used to heat water and run machines.

Wave Power

Ron Dahlquist/SuperStock

All day and all night, ocean waves are on the move. Scientists are working on ways to change the energy in waves into energy for homes and businesses. Ocean power is already being used in Canada and Scotland.

When we drive, watch TV, or even turn on lights, we are using energy. Most of our energy comes from burning oil, coal, and gas. When they burn, these energy sources pollute the air. We will probably run out of these energy sources some day. What can we use instead?

Wind, plants, the Sun's rays, and ocean waves are part of nature. They are also sources of energy. Energy from the Sun, wind, plants, and ocean waves is clean. Even better, we may not ever run out of them. —Lisa Jo Rudy

Wind Power

age fotostock/SuperStock

Wind farms are groups of windmills that turn the power of wind into energy. When wind turns the big blades of the windmills, wind power is turned into electricity. That electricity can be used to heat water, turn on lights, and power TVs, computers, and washing machines.

Plant Power

(t) Matthew Staver/UPI/Landov
(b) Jeffrey Sauger/Bloomberg News/Landov

Some kinds of plants can be used to make fuel for cars. This fuel is called biofuel, or ethanol. Sugarcane, corn, and sugar beets are examples of plants that can be used to make this kind of clean fuel.

Description Writing Frame

Use the Writing Frame below to orally summarize "Energy All Around."

Energy can be in **many interesting forms. For example,** _____

_____ for Earth.

Energy can also be stored in things **such as** _____

_____ .

Machines can change _____

_____ .

Moving energy can run things **such as** _____

_____ .

Our bodies use the stored energy in food. **For example**, when we

run we _____

_____ .

Energy can also be carried by waves, **such as** _____

_____ .

Use the frame to write the summary on another sheet of paper.
Be sure to include the **bold** signal words. Keep this as a model
of this Text Structure.

Critical Thinking

1 A substance that we burn for energy is called _____.

    A. fuel

    B. waves

    C. film

2 Point to the text that names sources of energy in "The Future of Energy."

3 Read aloud the sentences that tell about the energy of the wind in "The Future of Energy."

4 Talk about the photographs on pages 8–9 with a partner. How do they help you understand what you have read?

A photograph is a picture taken with a camera.

Digital Learning

For a list of links and activities that relate to this Science standard, visit the California Treasures Web site at www.macmillanmh.com to access the Content Reader resources.

Have children view the Science in Motion video "How You Hear."

EL In addition, distribute copies of the Translated Concept Summaries in Spanish, Chinese, Hmong, Khmer, and Vietnamese.

Energy and Matter

Scientists classify matter into three forms, or states: solids, liquids, or gases. Each of these states of matter has certain properties.

▲ The glass is a solid. The milk is a liquid.

Pencils, desks, pillows, and chairs are solids (SAHL•idz). A **solid** is matter that has a definite shape and **volume** (VAHL•yewm). **Volume** is the amount of space that an object takes up.

A **liquid** (LIK•wid) has definite volume but does not have a definite shape. A liquid takes the shape of its container. Water, oil, juice, and shampoo are liquids. They take the shape of their containers until poured into glasses or different containers.

A **gas** is matter that does not have definite shape or volume. Most gases are invisible. What happens when you blow into a balloon? The gas takes the shape of its container—the balloon. The gas spreads out and fills the balloon.

The gas that filled these balloons came from this small tank. Gases do not have a definite volume. They spread out and fill what they are in. ▶

Matter can change. A **physical change** (FIZ•i•kuhl CHAYNJ) is a change in the way matter looks even though the makeup of the matter has not changed. A **chemical change** (KEM•i•kuhl CHAYNJ) is a change that causes different kinds of matter to form. The properties of the new matter are different from those of the original substances. When you bake bread, you combine ingredients such as eggs and flour. The baked bread is a new substance with a taste that differs from the original materials of eggs and flour.

ingredients   dough   bread

When matter is heated, it gains heat energy. If enough heat energy is added, its state can change. When a solid gains enough heat energy, it will **melt**, or turn into a liquid. Ice cream melts after gaining only a small amount of heat energy. When a liquid gains heat energy, it will **evaporate** (i•VAP•uh•rayt), or turn into a gas. Water in wet clothes on a clothesline evaporates when the water droplets in the clothes gain heat energy from the sun and turn into a gas, or water vapor. The clothes become dry.

▲ When solid steel gains enough heat energy, it melts.

Water Troubles

Fresh, clean water is becoming even more precious for millions of people around the world.

Earth is about 75% water. But most of that water is salty. Only about 2.5% of Earth's water is fresh water—the kind we can drink and that plants need to grow. Much of Earth's fresh water is locked up in ice caps. In all, just 1% of Earth's water can be used for washing, drinking, cooking, and watering crops.

In the United States, we don't usually worry about having enough clean, fresh water. We turn on a faucet and there it is. We even play in it. In other countries, though, water is scarce. People in Africa, Asia, and Latin America have serious water shortages.

▲ In the U.S, kids play in clean, fresh water.

What causes water shortages? In some places, well water is being used faster than wells can refill. In other places, droughts— long periods without enough rain—mean there is not enough water. Some parts of the United States are now having water problems because of drought.

Evaporation is a big problem in some parts of the world. When the Sun shines on water, the water turns to vapor (gas) and rises into the air. The water is gone before it can do any good. The ground becomes dry and cracked. Nothing can grow.

◄ In some countries, there's no water to spare.

Anne Ackermann/Getty Images

Rao Guojun/ChinaFotoPress/Getty

14

Not all fresh water is safe to drink. Water in wells, lakes, and rivers may contain organisms that cause illness. Water can also be polluted by chemicals.

But the news isn't all bad. Mansoor Ali, who works for the United Nations, says water problems can be solved. Kids and adults are learning how to protect water and to use it wisely.

Karen Kasmauski/Corbis

▲ A boy drinks water from a lake in the country of Mali in Africa.

Clean Water Means Healthy Kids

When water is dirty, it can be dangerous to drink. In one school in Romania, old broken-down pipes made the water dirty. Dirty water was making children sick. It was dangerous to get a drink or even wash your hands. Then a Romanian aid group and the Earth Day Network came to help. They rebuilt the school's pipes and bathrooms. Now there's plenty of fresh water to drink and wash with. —*Kathryn Satterfield*

Kids to the Rescue

Three teenagers worked together to win an important prize for helping to solve the water problem!

Stockholm International Water Institute

▲ The winners!

Pontso Moletsane, Motobele Motschodi, and Sechaba Ramabenyane all grew up in South Africa. Together, they created a system to irrigate (water) crops using less water. How did they do it? They created a watering system that runs at night. The Sun doesn't shine at night, so less water evaporates. The new system will help South Africa save precious water.

Compare/Contrast Writing Frame

Use the Writing Frame below to orally summarize "Energy and Matter."

Solids, liquids and gases are **all** _____

_____ .

A solid and a liquid **both** have _____ ,

but **unlike** a solid, a liquid _____ .

A gas is **different** from a solid in that _____

_____ .

Matter is **similar** to a gas in that it can change. When a solid

gains heat energy, _____

_____ .

A liquid is **different**. When it gains heat energy, _____

_____ .

So, _____

are the **same** and **different**.

Use the frame to write the summary on another sheet of paper. Be sure to include the **bold** signal words. Keep this as a model of this Text Structure.

Critical Thinking

1 The amount of space that an object takes up is

   called _____.

   A. volume

   B. evaporation

   C. solid

2 Point out the sentences in "Energy and Matter" that compare and contrast a physical change with a chemical change.

3 Read aloud the text in this article that tells what happens to a liquid when it evaporates.

4 Describe for a partner what the diagram on page 13 shows.

A diagram is a drawing or a plan. It explains the parts of something or the way it works.

Digital Learning

For a list of links and activities that relate to this Science standard, visit the California Treasures Web site at www.macmillanmh.com to access the Content Reader resources.

Have children view the Science in Motion video "From Solid to Liquid to Gas."

EL In addition, distribute copies of the Translated Concept Summaries in Spanish, Chinese, Hmong, Khmer, and Vietnamese.

Elements and Atoms

What makes up matter? Ancient people decided that all matter was made up of earth, wind, fire, and water.

Today scientists use experiments and modern tools such as high-powered microscopes to observe matter. Today we know that all matter is made up of **elements** (EL•uh•munts). The **periodic table** (peer•ee•AH•dik TAY•buhl) lists the known elements. More than 100 different elements have been named. Some are named after places. *Californium* is named for California.

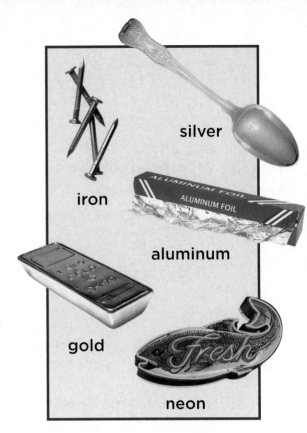

silver
iron
aluminum
gold
neon

▲ A few elements are shown here.

The Periodic Table of the Elements

Key

11 — Atomic number
Na — Element symbol
Sodium — Element name

☐ Metals
☐ Metalloids (semimetals)
☐ Nonmetals

1																	18
1 **H** Hydrogen	**2**											13	14	15	16	17	**30** **He** Helium
3 **Li** Lithium	**4** **Be** Beryllium											**5** **B** Boron	**6** **C** Carbon	**7** **N** Nitrogen	**8** **O** Oxygen	**9** **F** Fluorine	**10** **Ne** Neon
11 **Na** Sodium	**12** **Mg** Magnesium	3	4	5	6	7	8	9	10	11	12	**13** **Al** Aluminum	**14** **Si** Silicon	**15** **P** Phosphorus	**16** **S** Sulfur	**17** **Cl** Chlorine	**18** **Ar** Argon
19 **K** Potassium	**20** **Ca** Calcium	**21** **Sc** Scandium	**22** **Ti** Titanium	**23** **V** Vanadium	**24** **Cr** Chromium	**25** **Mn** Manganese	**26** **Fe** Iron	**27** **Co** Cobalt	**28** **Ni** Nickel	**29** **Cu** Copper	**30** **Zn** Zinc	**31** **Ga** Gallium	**32** **Ge** Germanium	**33** **As** Arsenic	**34** **Se** Selenium	**35** **Br** Bromine	**36** **Kr** Krypton
37 **Rb** Rubidium	**38** **Sr** Strontium	**39** **Y** Yttrium	**40** **Zr** Zirconium	**41** **Nb** Nioblum	**42** **Mo** Molybdenum	**43** **Tc** Technetium	**44** **Ru** Ruthenium	**45** **Rh** Rhodium	**46** **Pd** Palladium	**47** **Ag** Silver	**48** **Cd** Cadmium	**49** **In** Indium	**50** **Sn** Tin	**51** **Sb** Antimony	**52** **Te** Tellurium	**53** **I** Iodine	**54** **Xe** Xenon
55 **Cs** Cesium	**56** **Ba** Barium	**57** **La** Lanthanum	**72** **Hf** Hafnium	**73** **Ta** Tantalum	**74** **W** Tungsten	**75** **Re** Rhenium	**76** **Os** Osmium	**77** **Ir** Iridium	**78** **Pt** Platinum	**79** **Au** Gold	**80** **Hg** Mercury	**81** **Tl** Thallium	**82** **Pb** Lead	**83** **Bi** Bismuth	**84** **Po** Polonium	**85** **At** Astatine	**86** **Rn** Radon
87 **Fr** Francium	**88** **Ra** Radium	**89** **Ac** Actinium	**104** **Rf** Rutherfordium	**105** **Db** Dubnium	**106** **Sg** Seaborgium	**107** **Bh** Bohrium	**108** **Hs** Hassium	**109** **Mt** Meitnerium	**110** **Ds** Darmstadtium	**111** **Rg** Roentgenium	**Uub** Ununbium						

58 **Ce** Cerium	**59** **Pr** Praseodymium	**60** **Nd** Neodymium	**61** **Pm** Promethium	**62** **Sm** Samarium	**63** **Eu** Europium	**64** **Gd** Gadolinium	**65** **Tb** Terbium	**66** **Dy** Dysprosium	**67** **Ho** Holmium	**68** **Er** Erbium	**69** **Tm** Thulium	**70** **Yb** Ytterbium	**71** **Lu** Lutetium
90 **Th** Thorium	**91** **Pa** Protactinium	**92** **U** Uranium	**93** **Np** Neptunium	**94** **Pu** Plutonium	**95** **Am** Americium	**96** **Cm** Curium	**97** **Bk** Berkelium	**98** **Cf** Californium	**99** **Es** Einsteinium	**100** **Fm** Fermium	**101** **Md** Mendelevium	**102** **No** Nobelium	**103** **Lr** Lawrencium

Elements are made up of tiny particles called atoms (AT•uhmz). An **atom** is the smallest unit of an element that has the properties of that element. All atoms of a specific element are identical to each other.

Atoms are everywhere, but you cannot see them with the naked eye. Atoms cannot even be seen through most microscopes. Scientists study atoms with special instruments called *electron microscopes*. These high-powered tools help scientists learn about the tiniest bits of matter.

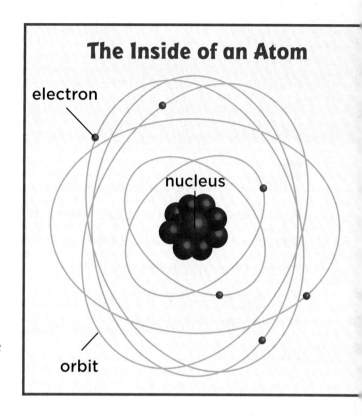

The Inside of an Atom

electron

nucleus

orbit

If you could compare the size of an atom to the size of an apple, this would be the same as comparing the size of an apple to the size of Earth. ▼

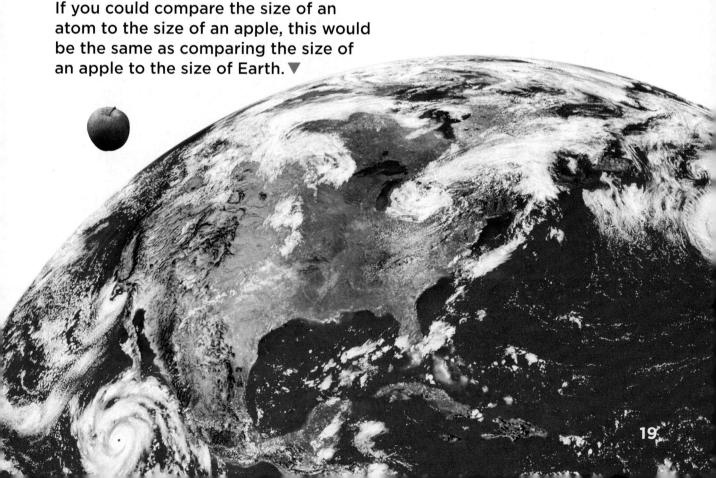

The Atomic Age

You might have heard of the Ice Age. But have you heard of the Atomic Age?

The Atomic Age gets its name from the atom. Atoms are the tiny particles of which all matter is made. They are too small to see with our eyes, but they are very important. Everything on Earth is made of atoms.

People have known about atoms for hundreds of years. At the end of the nineteenth century, scientists discovered that atoms can change. When atoms change, they release energy. That energy—called atomic energy—became important in the history of the world.

The Beginning of the Atomic Age

Most people say the Atomic Age began in the late 1930s, when scientists figured out how to get energy from atoms. Soon after, scientists figured out how to use atomic energy to make bombs.

People also say that the most important year in the Atomic Age was 1946. This was during World War II. The United States dropped two atomic bombs on Japan. Thousands of people were killed instantly. Thousands more died later. World War II soon ended.

▲ The U.S. used deadly atomic bombs to help end World War II.

Using Atomic Energy for Peaceful Purposes

After the war, during the 1950s, scientists got to work figuring out how to use atomic energy for peaceful purposes. This atomic energy—also called nuclear energy—could be used to make electricity. It could help doctors diagnose and treat some illnesses.

The Ford Motor Company thought cars might be able to run on atomic energy. In 1957 the company showed a model of an atomic-powered car, called the Nucleon. The Nucleon was never built. Using atomic energy in cars wasn't very practical.

By the 1960s the Atomic Age was over. People were worried that nuclear energy was not safe. It was still used to make electricity and in other important ways. But the excitement had died down.

The Future of Atomic Energy

Nuclear energy is still part of modern life. Scientists and businesses are taking another look at ways to use it safely to make clean energy. Maybe another Atomic Age is not too far off.

The Nucleon

Bettmann/Corbis

Nuclear power plants are an important source of energy today.

Peter Widmann/Alamy

Problem/Solution Writing Frame

Use the Writing Frame below to orally summarize "Elements and Atoms."

Ancient people had **trouble** figuring out what makes up matter.

To **solve their problem**, they decided that _____

_____ .

Today, scientists have **solved** the same **problem** by using _____

_____ .

As a result, scientists now know that _____ .

Without modern tools, scientists would not have discovered that matter is made up of elements. This is **because** elements are

made up of _____ .

Atoms are everywhere, but the **problem** is that _____

_____ .

Another **problem** is that _____

_____ .

As a result, _____ .

Use the frame to write the summary on another sheet of paper. Be sure to include the **bold** signal words. Keep this as a model of this Text Structure.

Critical Thinking

1 All matter is made up of _____.

    A. microscopes

    B. experiments

    C. elements

2 Show a partner where in "Elements and Atoms" to find the sentence that tells how many elements have been named.

3 Revisit pages 18 and 19. Read aloud the text that tells about electron microscopes.

A table presents a large amount of information, such as names and numbers, in a compact way.

4 Describe the table on page 18 to a partner.

Digital Learning

For a list of links and activities that relate to this Science standard, visit the California Treasures Web site at www.macmillanmh.com to access the Content Reader resources.

Have children view the e-Review "Building Blocks of Matter."

EL In addition, distribute copies of the Translated Concept Summaries in Spanish, Chinese, Hmong, Khmer, and Vietnamese.

Science

Shadows

How do you stay dry on a rainy day? You stand under an umbrella! The raindrops hit the open umbrella. They slide down its sides. Since the raindrops do not pass through the umbrella, they do not reach you.

Opaque (oh•PAYK) materials act somewhat like an umbrella to light energy. **Opaque** materials absorb some light energy. They reflect some of it as well. In this way, opaque objects block light energy from passing through them. Because the light energy is blocked, a **shadow**, or dark space, forms.

▼ Raindrops do not pass through the umbrella.

Opaque objects, such as a brick wall, a tree, a dog, or even you, do not let light pass through them. All opaque objects cast shadows. The shadows are formed on the opposite side of the light source.

Opaque materials can stop you from seeing objects behind them. Remember, you see an object when light that reflects from the object enters your eyes. Opaque materials block light, so you do not see the object.

▲ Shadows always form on the opposite side of a light source.

◄ Opaque objects block light from passing through them. This causes shadows to form.

Sunlight and Shadow

For thousands of years, the Sun has played an important part in where—and how—buildings are built.

Everyone who designs a building needs to understand sunlight and shadow.

The Sun and Stonehenge

Stonehenge is an ancient circle of stones built in the middle of a field in England. No one knows how the enormous stones got there or why they were placed the way they were. If you stand in the middle of the stone circle on most mornings, you won't notice anything special. But on the first official day of summer (called the summer solstice), which is the longest day of the year, the Sun rises behind one of the biggest stones. The Sun looks like a fiery ball balancing on the towering stone.

Whoever built Stonehenge knew a lot about the movement of the Sun. They also knew a lot about light and shadow.

Bill Bachmann/Photo Researchers, Inc.

The Sun rises over Stonehenge on the summer solstice.

Sunshine in Your Bedroom

The builders of Stonehenge weren't so different from today's architects—people with special training in how to design buildings. Architects think about light and shadow when they design houses, parks, skyscrapers, and even factories.

Architects know where the Sun rises and sets. If they were building a house in an empty field, they could make the bedroom face east for morning light. They could make the living room face west in the direction of sunsets.

Most of the time, though, architects design houses to fit into a neighborhood. They design skyscrapers to fit into a city. How do they know whether their buildings will block someone else's light? How do they know whether existing buildings, trees, or hills will make their new building too dark?

Architects build models that show the planned building and the buildings and structures around it. Sometimes they use computers to build the models, and sometimes they use cardboard and wood. The models help architects to figure out just how to place their building to get the most from the Sun. —*Lisa Jo Rudy*

Today, architects make models that show how sunlight and shadow will affect new buildings. ▼

Li Jiangsong/imaginechina/Zuma Press/Newscom

Cause/Effect Writing Frame

Use the Writing Frame below to orally summarize "Sunlight and Shadow."

Everyone who designs buildings needs to understand the **effect** of sunlight and shadow.

In an ancient circle of stones called Stonehenge, the Sun rises

behind one of the biggest stones **when** _____

_____ .

The **effect** of this is that _____

_____ .

Because of the **effect** of too much or too little sunlight,

architects must figure out _____

_____ .

Architects build models that show _____

_____ .

The **effect** of this is that architects place their buildings _____

_____ .

Use the frame to write the summary on another sheet of paper. Be sure to include the **bold** signal words. Keep this as a model of this Text Structure.

Critical Thinking

1   If a material can absorb some light energy, it is _____.

    A. opaque

    B. object

    C. rainy

2   Find the words in "Shadows" that define what a shadow is.

3   Point to the paragraph in "Shadows" about umbrellas. How are opaque materials like an umbrella?

4   With a partner, find the photographs on pages 24 and 25 that show shadows. Read each caption aloud.

A caption is a title or an explanation of a photograph.

Digital Learning

For a list of links and activities that relate to this Science standard, visit the California Treasures Web site at www.macmillanmh.com to access the Content Reader resources.

Have children view the e-Review "Shadows."

EL In addition, distribute copies of the Translated Concept Summaries in Spanish, Chinese, Hmong, Khmer, and Vietnamese.

Seeing Light and Color

Think about a ball that hits the ground bounces upward. Light acts much like this ball. When light hits an object, it bounces off in a different direction. Then it moves in a straight path. The bouncing of light waves off an object is called **reflection**.

Smooth, shiny surfaces, such as mirrors, reflect almost all the light that strikes them. This is because light bounces off these smooth surfaces in one direction, which allows for a clear picture, or image to form. When light hits a rough surface, it bounces off in different directions. A clear image can not form.

▲ Light is like a bouncing tennis ball. When it hits a surface, it bounces off in a new direction.

When light hits a smooth pond, the image on the surface is clear. When light hits a rough pond, the image is rough. ▼

The leaf looks green.

The flower looks red.

White light is made up of seven different colors of light. When white light strikes an object, some colors of light are **absorbed**, or taken in. Some colors of light are reflected. If you look at the object, some of the reflected light enters your pupils. You see the object as the color of this reflected light.

For example, white light that strikes a leaf is made up of seven different colors. The leaf absorbs all of the colors except for the green. Only green light bounces off the leaf. It is reflected to your eyes. You see the leaf as green. But when white light strikes a red flower, the green light is absorbed. Only the red light is reflected to your eyes. So you see the flower as red.

Searching the Skies

Richard Wainscoat/Alamy

Powerful Keck telescopes on Mount Mauna Kea in Hawaii

Mirrors and computers help us solve some of the mysteries of the universe.

How far can humans see into outer space? It all depends on how powerful our telescopes are.

A telescope's power depends largely on the size of the light-gathering mirror inside it. A huge, perfect mirror can capture the glow of a faint, faraway star. Today, the most powerful optical (or light-gathering) telescopes are the twin Keck telescopes on Mount Mauna Kea in Hawaii. The telescopes have light-gathering surfaces that are 32 feet across.

Until the Keck telescopes were built, the best telescopes had mirrors that were like thick glass hockey pucks. They were tough to make, very expensive, and extremely heavy. In the 1980s, scientists invented ways to make bigger but lighter mirrors. California astronomer Jerry Nelson designed the Keck's mirror. Instead of one big slab of glass, he used 36 smaller sheets that, under a computer's control, move as one. The Keck telescopes have already been used to discover many new planets.

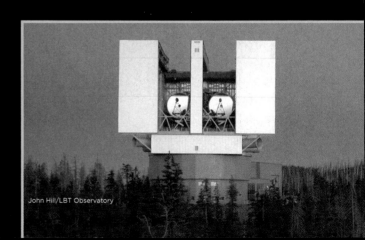

John Hill/LBT Observatory

In 2004, scientists started building an even more powerful telescope in Arizona. The Large Binocular Telescope (LBT) will cost $120 million. It will be able to look so far into space that it will see the beginnings of our universe.

Instead of using a lot of little mirrors, LBT will combine the light from two gigantic mirrors. In October 2005, LBT took its first image of space—what astronomers call first light— using just one mirror. —*Lisa Jo Rudy*

◀ **Seeing even deeper into the universe: the Large Binocular Telescope in Arizona**

How Mirrors Collect Light

The first telescopes used glass lenses to collect light. These telescopes had a problem: They broke the light from the stars into a rainbow, making it hard to see clearly. Isaac Newton, an English scientist, decided to try using a mirror inside a telescope instead.

Visual Arts Library (London)/Alamy

▲ **Isaac Newton's telescope**

In 1680, Newton built his first reflecting telescope. He used a curved, metal mirror to collect starlight. The mirror also reflected the light to a focus—the place where you put your eye to see the light.

Newton's design for the reflecting telescope is still used today. New types of mirrors with special coatings are used in ordinary smaller telescopes. Even an inexpensive reflector set up in the backyard is strong enough to show the craters of the Moon, the rings of Saturn, and the stars of the Milky Way galaxy.

NASA

Description Writing Frame

Use the Writing Frame below to orally summarize "Seeing Light and Color."

Light **has many interesting features**. It acts _____

_____ .

For example, when light hits an object, _____

_____ .

White light is made up of _____

_____ .

When white light strikes an object, _____

_____ .

For instance, when white light strikes a leaf, _____

_____ .

But when white light hits a red flower, _____

_____ .

Use the frame to write the summary on another sheet of paper. Be sure to include the **bold** signal words. Keep this as a model of this Text Structure.

Critical Thinking

1 When a color of light is taken in, it is _____.

    A. smooth

    B. bounced

    C. absorbed

2 Point to the sentence in "Searching the Skies" that tells what the power of a telescope depends on.

3 Find the sentences in this article that tell about Keck's mirror.

A diagram is a drawing or a plan. It explains the parts of something or the way it works.

4 What does the diagram on page 31 tell you? Discuss this with a partner.

Digital Learning

For a list of links and activities that relate to this Science standard, visit the California Treasures Web site at www.macmillanmh.com to access the Content Reader resources.

Have children view the Science in Motion video "Seeing Colors."

EL In addition, distribute copies of the Translated Concept Summaries in Spanish, Chinese, Hmong, Khmer, and Vietnamese.

Plants and Their Needs

From the tallest redwood tree to the smallest pansy, most plants have the same basic needs. They need water, sunlight, energy from food, and carbon dioxide. Carbon dioxide is a gas found in air. Plants need nutrients, too. Nutrients are substances that help living things grow and stay healthy. Plants must get all these things from their environment in order to survive.

Stems carry food and water throughout the plant. Stems also keep a plant upright so leaves can get sunlight.

Roots take in water and nutrients from the soil. They also keep a plant in place.

Plants have structures that help them get or make
what they need. A **structure** is a part of a living thing.
Most plants have roots, stems, and leaves. Many plants
also have flowers, fruits, and seeds. These parts help
plants live, grow, and reproduce. Reproduce means to
make new plants like themselves.

Leaves take in
carbon dioxide
from the air. They
use energy from
the Sun to
change carbon
dioxide and
water into food
for the plant.

This Flower Stinks!

People can't wait to see (and smell) one of the world's largest flowers.

Thousands of people couldn't wait to get to the Brooklyn Botanic Garden in New York. They wanted to see a rare flower called a titan arum. The gigantic plant was over five and a half feet tall. It's not the size the visitors will remember, though. The most amazing thing about the bloom of the titan arum is its smell. It's a terrible, awful, sickening smell. One whiff of the scent makes most people choke and hold their noses!

When titan arums bloom, the flowers put out an odor that smells like the rotting body of a dead animal. That's why many people call the plant by another name: corpse flower! The titan arum grows naturally in the country of Indonesia. The people there used to believe the plant would eat them!

David McNew/Newsmakers/Newscom

▲ Phew!

Creepy Baby

The gardeners at the Brooklyn Botanic Garden call their stinky plant Baby. Baby had been growing in Brooklyn for ten years, but it had never bloomed before. When it finally did, it was the first titan arum to bloom in New York City since 1939.

Before it bloomed, Baby grew more than 30 inches in just nine days. Some of the flowers can grow to nine feet tall. Scientists knew Baby was ready to open when it stopped growing. The huge blossom took about two hours to open. Then the bad, bad odor began to float through the air.

When this plant grows wild, its scent attracts beetles and bees. The titan arum's pollen sticks to their legs and bodies. When they fly to other plants, they carry the pollen with them. Plants need pollen from other plants of the same kind to produce new plants.

The stink from the titan arum is so strong, humans can smell it from over a half mile away. In Indonesia, some people dig up the rare plants to sell. This is against the law. The plant is also in trouble because its forest home is being destroyed. A lot of people hope they'll always have the chance to see and smell this stinky giant.

▲ In some places, titan arum's forest home is being destroyed.

REUTERS/Beawiharta/Newscom

Problem/Solution Writing Frame

**Use the Writing Frame below to orally summarize
"Plants and Their Needs"**

Most plants have the same basic needs. **Problems** begin when

these plants do not get _____.

Plants would also be in danger without nutrients **because**

_____.

But plants have structures that help them avoid **problems**.

The roots of a plant _____

_____.

The stems of plants _____

_____.

The leaves of plants _____

_____.

So, to avoid **problems**, grow, and stay healthy, plants get

what they need _____.

Use the frame to write the summary on another sheet of paper.
Be sure to include the **bold** signal words. Keep this as a model
of this Text Structure.

Critical Thinking

1 A part of a living thing is called a _____ .

    A. structure

    B. environment

    C. sunlight

2 Find the description of the titan arum in "This Flower Stinks!" Discuss this with a partner.

3 Point out the sentence or sentences in this article that tell what makes Baby different from most plants.

4 Use the diagram on pages 36 and 37 to show a partner how plants get what they need.

A diagram is a drawing or a plan. It explains the parts of something or the way it works.

Digital Learning

For a list of links and activities that relate to this Science standard, visit the California Treasures Web site at www.macmillanmh.com to access the Content Reader resources.

Have children view the Science e-Review "Living Things and Their Needs."

EL In addition, distribute copies of the Translated Concept Summaries in Spanish, Chinese, Hmong, Khmer, and Vietnamese.

Animals and What They Need

Like plants, all animals have the same basic needs. Animals need water, energy from food, and oxygen. Oxygen is a gas found in air and water. Animals need shelter and safety, too. A **shelter** is a place in which animals can stay safe.

Animals have structures that help them meet their needs in their environments. Body parts such as legs, wings, and beaks are examples of animal structures.

▲ Birds use nests for shelter.

Getting Food, Water, and Oxygen

Animals cannot make their own food the way plants can. Instead, they must eat plants or other animals. Legs, fins, and wings help animals move to find food. Beaks and tongues help animals catch and swallow food. They help animals drink water, too.

A lion's rough tongue helps it get water. ▶

42

Structures help animals breathe. Animals breathe to get oxygen. Many animals breathe with lungs. Lungs take in oxygen from the air. Fish breathe by pushing water through their gills. Gills take in oxygen from water.

gills

▲ Gills help fish get oxygen.

Finding Shelter and Staying Safe

Some animals use trees or other plants for shelter. Other animals build their own shelters. Birds, for example, build nests as shelters for their young. Birds use their beaks and feet to gather materials and build nests.

Some animals have structures that help them stay safe. A kangaroo's pouch helps young kangaroos stay safe. A porcupine's sharp quills help it to stay safe from other animals.

A young kangaroo develops in its mother's pouch. There it stays safe. ▶

43

Mighty Little Meerkats

A meerkat mob works together to survive in Africa's Kalahari Desert.

Meerkats live in one place on Earth—the Kalahari Desert in Africa. Life there is hard. Meerkats must be careful. Otherwise, they can end up as some other animal's snack.

Meerkats are furry little animals. They are only about one foot long. They aren't very strong. To stay alive, meerkats must work together. They help each other find food, raise young, and protect themselves.

Lunch! ▶

David Paynter/age fotostock/SuperStock

Member of the Mob

Up to 30 meerkats live together in a group called a mob or gang. Each meerkat mob keeps to its own area. Inside this area the mob builds a burrow in the desert sand. Meerkats search for food and water only in their territory.

▼ A mob of meerkats

age fotostock/SuperStock

Meerkats must leave the safety of the burrow during the day to look for food. They find insects in the sand. Their strong feet and claws dig out a meal of beetles or scorpions.

Share and Share Alike

Meerkats work together to look for food. Each day one meerkat is the lookout for the group. The lookout stands up on its two hind legs and watches. It uses sharp eyesight to look for animals that might attack. Now the other meerkats can safely hunt. When the lookout spots danger, it barks loudly. That's the signal to get away—fast! The meerkats run for the nearest burrow and dive in. Sometimes they can't escape. Then a whole mob might face an enemy together. The group can sometimes scare off a much larger animal.

Meerkats even stay close to each other at night. The animals hug each other before going to sleep. Now that's togetherness! —*Curtis Slepian*

Body of Information

This two-pound animal has a lot of ways to survive in the desert.

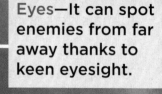

Eyes—It can spot enemies from far away thanks to keen eyesight.

Ears—It can close its ears to keep out the desert sand.

Nose—A strong sense of smell leads it to insects under the sand.

Fur—Its brown color lets it blend in with sand and rocks.

Tail—It uses it as a third leg, to balance itself when upright.

Feet—Powerful front claws dig through hundreds of pounds of sand each day.

Nigel J. Dennis; Gallo Images/CORBIS

45

Problem/Solution Writing Frame

Use the Writing Frame below to orally summarize "Animals and What They Need."

All Animals have the same basic needs. **Problems** begin when

animals do not get _____ .

To help **solve the problem** of getting what they need, animals

have _____ .

One **problem** that animals have, but that plants do not, is that

_____ .

Animals must _____

_____ .

Most animals also have the **problem** of _____

_____ .

Some animals **solve** this **problem** by _____

_____ .

Other animals _____ .

Use the frame to write the summary on another sheet of paper.
Be sure to include the **bold** signal words. Keep this as a model
of this Text Structure.

Critical Thinking

1 A place in which animals can stay safe is called a _____.

   A. shelter

   B. structure

   C. pouch

2 Read the sentences in "Mighty Little Meerkats" that describe meerkats.

3 Point out the sentence in "Mighty Little Meerkats" that tells what meerkats do before going to sleep. How is this an example of togetherness?

4 Talk about the caption that goes with the photograph of the fish on page 43. Tell a partner what the caption says about the fish.

A caption is a title or an explanation of a photograph.

Digital Learning

For a list of links and activities that relate to this Science standard, visit the California Treasures Web site at www.macmillanmh.com to access the Content Reader resources.

Have children view the e-Review "Living Things and Their Needs."

EL In addition, distribute copies of the Translated Concept Summaries in Spanish, Chinese, Hmong, Khmer, and Vietnamese.

Living Things in Different Environments

An **adaptation** (ad•uhp•TAY•shun) is a special feature or behavior that helps a living thing survive in its environment.

Arctic tundra plants have adaptations such as shallow roots to help them survive in mostly frozen soil. And most plants grow close to the ground to protect them from the cold and wind.

Many forest trees have adapted to grow tall, toward the light. Plants on the forest floor often have large leaves to soak in as much light as possible.

Plants in wetland areas have tubes in their stems that carry oxygen from their leaves to their roots.

Nearly all grassland grasses have adapted to grow in dry conditions. Their deep roots soak up moisture.

In the ocean, **algae** (AL•jee), which are plantlike living things, have no roots. This adaptation allows them to drift near the sunlit surface of the water.

▲ This desert plant has waxy skin and thick leaves adapted to store water.

Grasses and reeds grown in wetlands. ▶

48

Animals adapt, too. Many desert animals sleep all day and come out when it is cooler. Others have special features that help them stay cool.

Animals in the wetlands have adapted to living in water. Some breathe through their skin.

Many arctic tundra animals have thick coats and layers of fat to keep them warm. Others have wide and furry feet to help them run in snow.

Some grassland animals have flat teeth for eating grasses. Small animals have adapted ways to hide.

▲ Zebras use their flat teeth to bite grass.

Animals in forests where the seasons change eat extra food, grow thicker coats, or go to sleep to keep warm during cold winters.

Some ocean animals have a body part called gills. Gills get oxygen from water.

1 Water enters the fish's mouth.

2 The gills take in oxygen from the water.

A Whole New World

Scientists discover new species on land and in the sea.

Gerry Allen/Conservation International

A colorful new species

There's still plenty to explore and discover on Earth.

Treasures Under the Sea

Fish that change color in seconds and sharks that walk. These are just two examples of the new species of undersea life found in part of the Indian Ocean. The area is off the coast of Papua New Guinea, in Indonesia.

A 12-member team of scientists from the organization called Conservation International identified 24 new species of fish, 20 species of coral, and 8 species of shrimp. All of these discoveries were made within a 6-week period in one part of the ocean.

Two types of sharks, called epaulette sharks, were discovered. These 3-foot-long spotted fish live in shallow water. They use their lower fins to walk on the sea bottom!

This shark walks on the ocean floor. ▼

Gerry Allen/Conservation International

TIME
FOR KIDS

▲ This is what scientists think the new mammal looks like.

New Land Creatures, Too

Scientists on land are also making the same kind of discoveries. A team from the World Wildlife Fund (WWF) thinks it has found a new animal in the rain forests of Borneo. Borneo is a large island divided among the countries of Malaysia, Indonesia, and Brunei.

The mysterious creature looks like a cross between a cat and a fox. It has dark red fur, a long, bushy tail, small ears, and large hind legs. Researchers set up cameras in the rain forest. They got two pictures of the animal at night.

Biologist Stephan Wulffraat said, "We have consulted with several Bornean wildlife experts. Some thought it looked like a lemur. But most were convinced it was a new species of carnivore."

A carnivore is an animal that eats other animals. "Until we have a live specimen in our hands, we can't be 100 percent sure," Wulffraat said.

The WWF is racing against time to find the new catlike animal. Its home may eventually be destroyed. Indonesia has plans to build a palm oil plantation in the rain forest where it was photographed. —*Claudia Atticot*

Cause/Effect Writing Frame

Use the Writing Frame below to orally summarize "Living Things in Different Environments."

Adaptation helps a living thing survive in its environment.

Some desert plants have thick leaves **because** _____

_____ .

Mostly frozen soil has **caused** arctic tundra plants to

_____ .

If a tree in the forest has grown tall, **then** you know that it has

_____ .

If grasses grow deep roots that soak up moisture, **then** you

know that _____ .

Living in the wetlands has **caused** some animals to

_____ .

Therefore, the **effect** of adaptation is _____

_____ .

Use the frame to write the summary on another sheet of paper.
Be sure to include the **bold** signal words. Keep this as a model
of this Text Structure.

Critical Thinking

1 Plantlike living things in the ocean are called _____.

    A. animals

    B. adaptations

    C. algae

2 Point out where in "A Whole New World" the text describes epaulette sharks.

3 Read aloud the sentences in "A Whole New World" that tell about a possible new species of carnivore on Borneo.

4 Describe for a partner what the diagram on page 49 shows.

A diagram is a drawing or a plan. It explains the parts of something or the way it works.

Digital Learning

For a list of links and activities that relate to this Science standard, visit the California Treasures Web site at www.macmillanmh.com to access the Content Reader resources.

Have children view the Science in Motion video "Adaptations of Desert Plants."

EL In addition, distribute copies of the Translated Concept Summaries in Spanish, Chinese, Hmong, Khmer, and Vietnamese.

How Do Living Things Change Their Environments?

Every living thing changes it's environment in some way. Some living things make small changes. A spider spins a web. A bird builds a nest. A squirrel buries an acorn. All these actions change the environment in small ways.

Living things can also change their environments in more noticeable ways. Bacteria, worms, and fungi live in the soil. They break down leaves and other dead plant material. They help add nutrients back to the soil. These living things make big changes that help the environment.

Competition (kahm•pi•TISH•uhn) can be a major cause of change. **Competition** is the struggle among living things for food, water, and other needs.

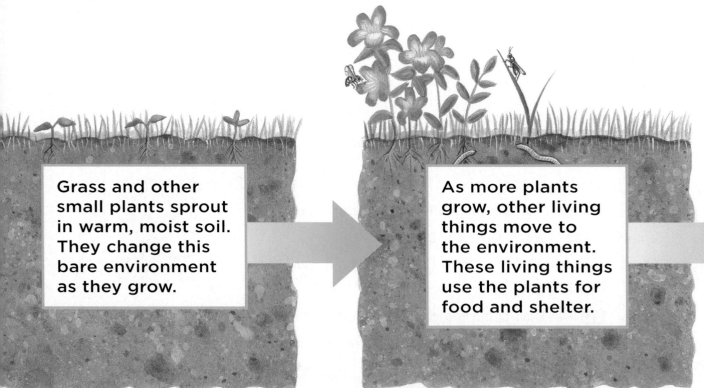

Grass and other small plants sprout in warm, moist soil. They change this bare environment as they grow.

As more plants grow, other living things move to the environment. These living things use the plants for food and shelter.

As grass begins to grow, it takes in nutrients and water from the soil. It changes the environment as it meets its needs. In time, animals eat the grass for food. These animals change the environment as they meet their needs. When shrubs and trees begin to grow, they compete for space, light, and water. The trees block sunlight from reaching the smaller plants. The smaller plants may die. In this way environments change as living things compete to meet their needs.

When shrubs take root, more animals move to the environment. The plants and animals compete to meet their needs.

In time, trees grow and the environment continues to change.

Going, Going, Gone?

Extinction can be a natural process. It can also be caused by human actions.

Eighty kinds of birds have died out in the last 300 years. Some became extinct due to natural causes. Others died out when people destroyed their habitat.

Check out the stories of two extinct birds. They can teach us a lot about what people can do to protect other living things.

The Dodo

Dodos were first seen around 1600. Sailors spotted them on the island of Mauritius in the Indian Ocean. The plump dodo was a perfect meal for sailors and the animals they brought with them. The clumsy birds were easy prey because they could not fly. The visitors also cut down much of the island's forests for wood.

Without the trees, the dodo lost its home and source of food. Less than 80 years after the first sailors arrived, the dodo was extinct.

◄ The dodo has been extinct for almost 400 years.

Photo Researchers

The Carolina Parakeet

This colorful bird was the only parrot native to the eastern United States. The largest ones were 13 inches long. Carolina parakeets once lived all over the southeastern United States. They were fruit eaters. Farmers thought of them as hungry pests. The birds were also hunted for their beautiful feathers. They became extinct in the 1920s. —*Lisa Jo Rudy*

Steven Holt-Courtesy of ANSP/Picturedesk International/Newscom

California's Endangered Species

There are hundreds of threatened and endangered plants and animals in California. When living things are labeled "threatened" or "endangered," the government may protect them. Then, people can't hunt them or harm them.

Here are some endangered animals in California:

- Sea lion
- Sperm whale
- Wolverine
- Sea otter
- California condor
- Northern spotted owl
- California pelican
- Green, loggerhead, leatherback, and olive ridley sea turtles
- Desert tortoise

Wolverine

fl online/Alamy

Richard Mittleman/ Gon2Foto/Alamy

California condor

57

Sequence Writing Frame

**Use the Writing Frame below to orally summarize
"How Do Living Things Change Their Environments?"**

Every living thing changes its environment over time.

After bacteria, worms, and fungi become part of soil, _____

_____ .

Next, they _____

_____ .

At the **same time** that grass grows, _____

_____ .

Then _____ .

At the **same time** that shrubs grow, they compete for space,

light, and water. First the trees _____

_____ .

Then, the smaller plants _____

_____ .

Use the frame to write the summary on another sheet of paper.
Be sure to include the **bold** signal words. Keep this as a model
of this Text Structure.

Critical Thinking

1   The struggle among living things for food, water, and other

needs is called _____.

    A. competition

    B. change

    C. nutrients

2   Reread the paragraph in "Going, Going, Gone?" that tells about dodo birds.

3   Show a partner which paragraph in "Going, Going, Gone?" tells about a colorful bird that became extinct in the 1920s.

4   Use the list on page 57 to talk about endangered animals in California.

> A list is a series of names or items put in a meaningful sequence or grouping.

Digital Learning

For a list of links and activities that relate to this Science standard, visit the California Treasures Website at www.macmillanmh.com to access the Content Reader resources.

Have children view the Science in Motion video, "A Changing Environment."

EL In addition, distribute copies of the Translated Concept Summaries in Spanish, Chinese, Hmong, Khmer, and Vietnamese.

Changes Affect Plants

When an environment changes, the plants adapted to that environment can be harmed. Some plants have adaptations that help them survive. Living things that are not able to change might die.

Living things can change their environment. Weather and other things can also change environments. Lightning might start a grassland or forest fire. Too much rain might cause flooding.

Wild flowers in Anza Borrego State Park, California, bloom quickly after a spring rain.

▲ Mount St. Helens, a volcano in Washington, erupted in 1980. This eruption knocked down or scorched trees on nearly 230 square miles of forest. The environment is slowly changing as new plants start to grow.

Some changes last a short time. A summer **drought**, or period of dry weather, can turn a green meadow brown. Spring rain can make a desert bloom with flowers. Earthquakes, storms, and volcanic eruptions can cause sudden changes in an environment. This damage can last for years.

Some living things can recover from harmful changes in their environment. Grassland grasses have roots that store food and moisture. The grasses survive and grow back quickly after a fire. However, trees may take hundreds of years to grow back after a fire.

People often cause permanent changes. When large trees in old forests are cut down, those trees are gone forever. Rivers and lakes polluted by trash or chemicals may not recover unless people clean them up.

The Heat Is On!

How will global warming affect crops and other living things?

Recent years have been some of the warmest ever. Of course, nature has caused big changes in Earth's climate in the past. The Ice Age was a natural change in climate. But most scientists now agree that humans are causing global warming.

Human-made Climate?

An atmosphere made of air and other gases surrounds Earth. Earth's atmosphere naturally traps heat from the Sun. It works much like a glass greenhouse, which warms the air inside even when temperatures outside are cool. This "greenhouse effect" makes life possible on our planet.

Too much greenhouse gas, though, can overheat Earth. When we burn fuels like coal and oil, we add greenhouse gases to the atmosphere. Kevin Trenberth of the National Center for Atmospheric Research says, "We are already seeing fewer frost days, heavier rains, and more droughts and heat waves."

The Natural Greenhouse Effect

Most of the Sun's heat goes back into space.

SUNLIGHT

HEAT

Earth's Atmosphere

Pollution's Impact

Most of the Sun's heat is trapped.

HEAT

What Will Happen to Plants?

Higher temperatures could affect where important crops like wheat and corn can be grown. In some areas, such as Canada and Russia, warmer weather will mean longer growing seasons and better harvests. In other areas, such as the southern United States, the weather may be too hot. Harvests may be small. Crops can also suffer if there is too much rain or if winds from strong storms damage the plants.

AGStockUSA, Inc./Alamy

▲ A healthy cornfield

What Will Happen to Animals?

Some animals, such as the polar bear, could lose their homes when ice sheets melt. Warmer waters will also make it harder for seals, seabirds, and other animals to find cold-water food called krill.

Melting ice sheets at the North and South Poles could add a lot more water to the oceans. The oceans could rise, swallowing coasts and low-lying islands where people live.

What Can Be Done?

The best chance to slow global warming is to reduce greenhouse gases. Some countries have agreed to do this. They signed a treaty called the Kyoto Protocol. So far, the United States has not signed. One thing is certain. If we really want to slow global warming, the whole world must help. —*David Bjerklie*

AP Photo/Topeka Capital Journal, Chris Landsberger

▲ An ear of corn hurt by bad weather

Cause/Effect Writing Frame

Use the Writing Frame below to orally summarize "Changes Affect Plants."

When an environment changes, the plants that adapted to it can be harmed.

Weather can **affect** plants. Lightning might **cause** _____

_____ .

Too much rain can **cause** _____

_____ .

A period of dry weather can **cause** _____

_____ .

A spring rain can **cause** _____ .

People can **cause** permanent changes. When large trees are cut

down, _____

_____ .

Therefore, the **effect** of change _____

_____ .

Use the frame to write the summary on another sheet of paper.
Be sure to include the **bold** signal words. Keep this as a model
of this Text Structure.

Critical Thinking

1 A period of dry weather is called a _____.

    A. fire

    B. drought

    C. desert

2 Find the sentence in "Changes Affect Plants" that names three things that cause sudden changes.

3 Read aloud the sentence in "The Heat Is On!" that tells what most scientists agree on. Talk about this with a partner.

4 What does the caption on page 61 describe? Read this caption aloud to a partner.

> A caption is a title or an explanation of a photograph.

Digital Learning

For a list of links and activities that relate to this Science standard, visit the California Treasures Web site at www.macmillanmh.com to access the Content Reader resources.

Have children view the e-Review "Changes Affect Living Things."

EL In addition, distribute copies of the Translated Concept Summaries in Spanish, Chinese, Hmong, Khmer, and Vietnamese.

Changes Affect Animals

When an environment changes, the animals adapted to that environment can be harmed. If the changes last a long time, some animals may move to a new habitat. Some animals find a way to survive by changing their behavior.

Like plants, animals have adaptations that help them survive in their environments. Zebras have flat teeth for chewing grass. Fish have gills that help them get oxygen from water. What would happen to a zebra if its **habitat**, or home, became too dry for a long time? What would happen to the living things in a pond if their habitat dried up?

◀ Animals such as this springbok depend on watering holes.

When there is no rain for a long time in the savanna, grasses can dry up. Watering holes can dry up, too. Zebras and other animals move to new habitats where they can find food and water. Frogs burrow in the mud. They will come out when rain falls again. But fish in a pond or lake can not move. If their habitat goes dry, they may die.

▲ Animals migrate, or move to another place, in search of food, water, and shelter as their habitat goes through changes.

◀ Many frogs are adapted to burrow and survive underground when the environment becomes dry.

TROUBLE in the Ocean

What's causing "dead zones" in oceans around the world?

The world's oceans are filled with life. But it's land-living human beings who are creating "dead zones" in coastal waters.

Over the past 40 years, dead zones have appeared in almost 150 places around the globe. Some are small, and some are vast. The dead zone in the Gulf of Mexico is as big as the state of New Jersey!

No animals live in these areas. There are no fish, no turtles, no crabs. The reason is that the water below the surface has no oxygen in it. Without oxygen, fish and other sea creatures die.

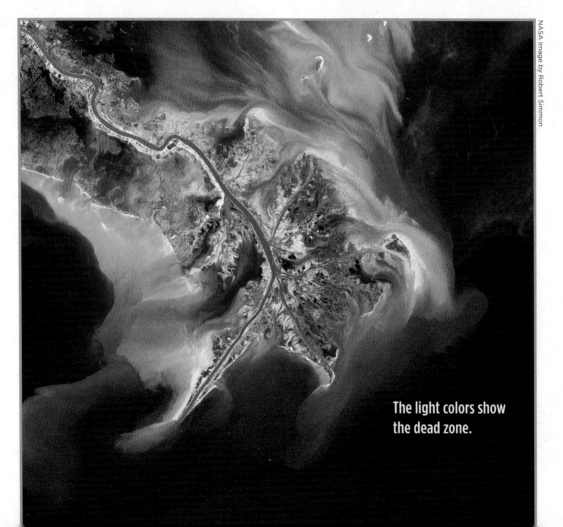

NASA Image by Robert Simmon

The light colors show the dead zone.

Too Much of a Good Thing

We know what causes dead zones—chemical fertilizers used on farms and lawns. The fertilizer helps plants and grass grow. But in the ocean, fertilizer is deadly.

When it rains, fertilizer chemicals wash into rivers. Rivers flow into an ocean. The chemicals are dumped there.

Now the fertilizer helps tiny plants called algae to grow. Soon the surface of the ocean is covered with algae for hundreds of miles. When the algae die, they sink to the bottom. There, bacteria eat them. The bacteria use up all the oxygen in the water. Once the oxygen is gone, nothing can live.

Robert Brook/Photo Researchers, Inc.

▲ Green algae on the ocean surface

Saving the Ocean

Governments around the world are trying to stop dead zones from forming. One solution is to plant trees and grass next to rivers. The plants will soak up fertilizer before it reaches the ocean. Another important solution is to use less or stop using chemical fertilizers altogether.

69

Cause/Effect Writing Frame

Use the Writing Frame below to orally summarize "Changes Affect Animals."

When an environment changes, the animals that adapted to that environment can be harmed.

If the changes last a long time, **then** _____.

And, if the changes last a long time, **then** _____.

For example, if there is no rain, it can **affect** animals. Watering

holes that dry up can **cause** _____

_____.

Dried-up watering holes can also **cause** _____

_____.

If a habitat for fish stays dry for too long, **then** _____

_____.

Therefore, the **effect** of change _____

_____.

Use the frame to write the summary on another sheet of paper. Be sure to include the **bold** signal words. Keep this as a model for writing a summary of this Text Structure.

Critical Thinking

1　Another name for a home is _____.

    A. mud

    B. harm

    C. habitat

2　Find the sentences in "Trouble in the Ocean" that tell why an area is called a dead zone.

3　Point to the sentences in the same article that tell about one solution to dead zones.

4　Discuss with a partner the photograph of the elephants on page 67. Describe what they are doing.

> A photograph is a picture taken with a camera.

Digital Learning

For a list of links and activities that relate to this Science standard, visit the California Treasures Web site at www.macmillanmh.com to access the Content Reader resources.

Have children view the e-Review "Changes Affect Living Things."

EL In addition, distribute copies of the Translated Concept Summaries in Spanish, Chinese, Hmong, Khmer, and Vietnamese.

When the Environment Suddenly Changes

Did you know that mammoths once lived in North America? They were closely related to elephants that live in Africa and Asia today. What happened? Why did the mammoths disappear?

Ten thousand years ago, North America was in an ice age. Sheets of ice covered much of the United States. Large animals, such as mammoths and saber-toothed cats, lived in this cold environment. Then the climate changed. Temperatures began to rise, and the ice started to melt. The plants that mammoths ate disappeared. The mammoths became extinct. **Extinct** means that there are no more of a type of living thing alive.

◄ Scientist think hunting is one reason woolly mammoths disappeared. Climate change is another reason.

Responding to Change

Change	Living Thing	What Might Happen	Why
warmer climate	saber-toothed cat	becomes extinct	unable to find food; unable to survive in warm climate
volcanic eruption	short-tailed albatross	survives	flies to new environment
colder climate	bear	survives	grows thicker fur

Climate change may cause populations to become extinct. Disease and human activities may also cause populations to become extinct. When a new population moves into an ecosystem, a whole community can be in danger. Some populations can survive sudden changes such as these. Other populations cannot.

This Croc Really Rocks

A fossil found in Africa tells of a giant crocodile that lived 110 million years ago.

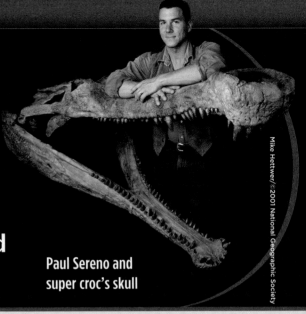

Paul Sereno and super croc's skull

Mike Hettwer/©2001 National Geographic Society

Paul Sereno knows what it's like to go into croc shock. In the year 2000, the dinosaur hunter was in Africa, in the country of Niger. There he dug up the bones of a huge crocodile. This super croc is now extinct. It lived about 105 million years before early humans were around. The last of its kind died out about 110 million years ago.

But while it lived, the super croc had plenty of dinosaurs to keep it company—and to eat.

How Big Was Super Croc?

The super croc was 40 feet long. That's as long as a school bus. It weighed as much as a small whale and had jaws about five feet long! What's more, the croc that Sereno found wasn't even fully grown. He thinks it probably took between 50 and 60 years for a super croc to grow to its full size.

Scientists say the super croc belonged to a species known as "flesh crocodile emperor." It's a good name for the giant, ferocious meat-eater.

Mike Hettwer/©2001 National Geographic Society

◀ Super croc's teeth

Built for Battle

The king of crocs ruled the African river, where it lived and hunted. It was built like a fighting machine. Armor-like bony plates covered the head, body, and part of the tail. The plates helped protect the croc from attacks. Its long, narrow jaw held more than 100 teeth.

"This thing could have easily pulled down a good-size dinosaur," Sereno said.

The super croc could lie underwater while watching the shore. The crocodile would wait for prey to approach, then chomp down with its teeth! It would drag its dinner into the water and drown it. —*Bill Doyle*

Sizing 'Em Up

Alligators and crocodiles belong to the same group of reptiles. They're all called crocodilians. When it comes to size, the modern versions don't measure up to their super croc ancestor.

Name: *Sarcosuchus imperator*
Habitat: The rivers of central Africa
Weight: About 17,500 pounds
Length: Up to 50 feet

Portia Sloan/National Geographic Society

E.R. Degginger/Bruce Coleman

Name: Australian crocodile
Habitat: Saltwater and freshwater areas in northern Australia and Asia
Weight: About 2,000 pounds
Length: Up to 23 feet

Name: American alligator
Habitat: Freshwater swamps and lakes in southeastern U.S.
Weight: 1,300 pounds
Length: Up to 20 feet

M.H. Sharp/Photo Researchers

Problem/Solution Writing Frame

**Use the Writing Frame below to orally summarize
"When the Environment Suddenly Changes."**

Ten thousand years ago, when North America was in an
ice age, mammoths lived.

When the climate changed, they had a **problem** because _____

_____ .

This led to another **problem** for mammoths. _____

_____ .

The mammoths started to die, and in time _____

_____ .

When a new population moves into an ecosystem, **then** _____

_____ .

Some populations find **solutions** or ways to survive sudden

changes, but _____

_____ .

Use the frame to write the summary on another sheet of paper.
Be sure to include the **bold** signal words. Keep this as a model
of this Text Structure.

Critical Thinking

1   If there are no more of a type of living thing alive, then that thing is _____.

    A. disappearing

    B. extinct

    C. environment

2   Show a partner where in "This Croc Really Rocks" a super croc is first described.

3   Read aloud the text in this article that gives information about a super croc's length and weight.

4   Describe the chart on page 73 to a partner.

A chart is a drawing that shows information in the form of a table, graph, or picture.

Digital Learning

For links and activities that relate to this Science standard, visit the California Treasures Web site at www.macmillanmh.com to access the Content Reader resources.

Have children view the Science e-Review "Living Things of the Past."

EL In addition, distribute copies of the Translated Concept Summaries in Spanish, Chinese, Hmong, Khmer, and Vietnamese.

Discovering the Solar System

A star is a hot, glowing ball of gases. The Sun is a medium-size star. We see other stars as tiny points of light in the night sky because they are very far away.

Look at the night sky on a clear evening. Choose a group of stars, or **constellation**. Make a drawing to help you remember what they look like and where they are. Check the sky again after one hour. Why are the stars not in the same place? Remember that Earth rotates on its axis.

The stars did not move. They only appeared to move because of the rotation of Earth. As Earth revolves around the Sun, we see different stars.

In the winter, you cannot see the stars that were in the summer sky. These stars are now on the opposite side of our orbit. In summer, you have moved to the other side of the Sun. So you cannot see constellations you saw in the winter in the summer sky at night.

▼ Can you see the constellation Orion in the summer night sky?

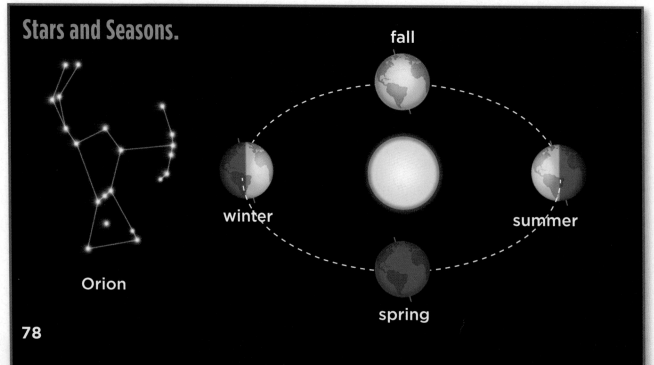

Stars and Seasons.

fall

winter

summer

spring

Orion

light from stars

path of light

lens

eyepiece

The stars, the planets, and the Moon are very far away. How do scientists learn about them? Scientists use telescopes (TEL•uh•skohps) to study distant objects in space. A **telescope** is a tool that gathers light to make faraway objects appear larger, closer, and clearer. The number of planets and stars that can be seen though a telescope is much greater than the number that can be seen by unaided eyes.

One of the best places for a telescope is in space. The Hubble Space Telescope travels around Earth. It takes pictures and sends them back to Earth. It can see objects in space more clearly than telescopes on Earth can.

Scientists study space with other kinds of telescopes, too. For example, radio telescopes collect radio waves. We cannot see radio waves. Scientists use computers to turn radio waves into pictures. That is how they learn about objects in space that we cannot see.

radio telescope

Eyes in the Sky

The Hubble Space Telescope has helped scientists see deep into the universe.

It wasn't easy to put the Hubble Space Telescope into orbit around Earth. It cost $2 billion and took a lot of hard work. Then, as soon as it was in orbit in 1990, astronomers found a problem. The mirror that made the telescope work was flawed. Astronauts had to fix it. The Space Shuttle got them there. Then they took a risky space walk to replace the Hubble's mirror.

Why did the United States put so much time, money, and effort into a telescope in space?

▲ An astronaut works on replacing Hubble's mirror.

Hubble's position outside Earth's atmosphere gives it a crystal-clear view of space. The gases that make up Earth's atmosphere interfere with our view of space from the ground. Even the best ground telescopes can't see clearly. Hubble can see more than any other telescope.

What's Up with Hubble?

Hubble is a telescope, and it uses its cameras to take pictures. But Hubble can do much more. Its special equipment allows Hubble to "see" objects that are invisible to human eyes.

Since it has been in orbit, Hubble has snapped about 500,000 images of more than 25,000 celestial objects. It has made 100,000 trips around Earth. Every day Hubble collects a huge amount of data. It sends the information back to astronomers on Earth. Already, Hubble has changed the way we think of the universe.

What's Next for Hubble?

Scientists don't know exactly how long Hubble can keep working. They'll do everything they can to keep its eyes looking deep into space for as long as possible. What will they discover? Stay tuned to find out! —*Lisa Jo Rudy*

Top Hubble Discoveries

* In our solar system, Hubble spotted two new moons orbiting Pluto.

* In the middle of our galaxy, the Milky Way, Hubble has found more than 15 Jupiter-size planets.

* Hubble took pictures that helped astronomers learn more about what happens to exploding stars.

* Hubble helped astronomers figure out that the universe is probably about 13.7 billion years old.

* Hubble found proof that black holes really exist.

▼ The birth of stars, photographed by Hubble

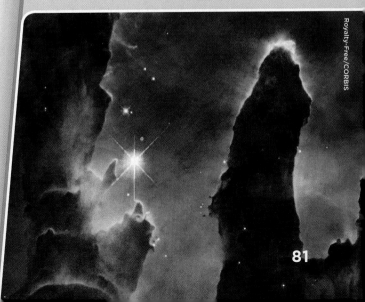

Royalty-Free/CORBIS

Compare/Contrast Writing Frame

**Use the Writing Frame below to orally summarize
"Discovering the Solar System."**

Stars have **many interesting features**. Stars are all the **same** in that

_____

_____ .

The Sun is a star. **However, unlike** other stars, _____

_____ .

Telescopes have **many interesting features**. Telescopes are the **same**

in that _____

_____ .

The Hubble Space Telescope is **unlike** most telescopes because

_____

_____ .

Radio telescopes are **different** from the Hubble telescope because

_____ .

Use the frame to write the summary on another sheet of paper.
Be sure to include the **bold** signal words. Keep it as a model
of this Text Structure.

Critical Thinking

1 A group of stars is called a _____ .

    A. telescope

    B. planet

    C. constellation

2 Point out the sentence in "Eyes in the Sky" that explains the problem astronomers found.

3 With a partner, read aloud the parts of the text from "Eyes in the Sky" that tell what Hubble can do.

4 Describe for a partner what the diagram on page 78 shows.

> A diagram is a drawing or a plan. It explains the parts of something or the way it works.

Digital Learning

For a list of links and activities that relate to this Science standard, visit the California Treasures Web site at www.macmillanmh.com to access the Content Reader resources.

Have children view the e-Review "What Is a Telescope?"

EL In addition, distribute copies of the Translated Concept Summaries in Spanish, Chinese, Hmong, Khmer, and Vietnamese.

The Moon's Shape

Like Earth, the Moon is shaped like a ball, or sphere. The Moon's shape does not change. It is always a sphere. Why then does the Moon look different each night?

The Moon, like Earth, moves through space. The Moon orbits Earth, much like Earth orbits the Sun. The Moon's shape seems to change because of this orbit. Look at the diagram. One half of the Moon faces the Sun and is lighted by the Sun. The other half faces away from the Sun and is in darkness. The Moon does not make its own light. As the Moon orbits Earth, we see different parts of it lighted. These lighted parts are the different shapes, or phases, we see.

It takes the Moon about four weeks to orbit Earth. During this time it passes through all of its phases. The four-week cycle of changing phases is called the **lunar cycle** (LEW•nuhr•SIGH•kuhl).

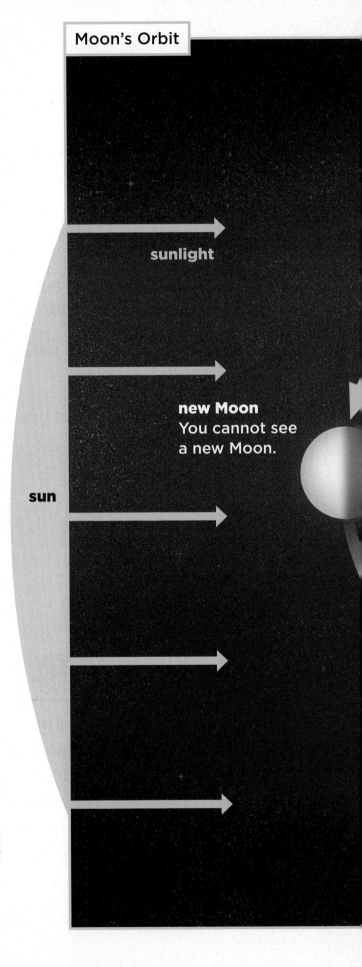

Moon's Orbit

sunlight

sun

new Moon
You cannot see a new Moon.

84

third quarter Moon.
Our view of the
Moon from Earth
21 days after the
new Moon.

full Moon.
Our view of the
Moon from Earth
14 days after the
new Moon.

first quarter Moon.
Our view of the Moon
from Earth 7 days
after the new Moon.

Eight Is Enough

Astronomers decide Pluto cannot be called a planet.

Jerry LoFaro

▲ Pluto and two of its moons

Poor, puny Pluto! After it was discovered in 1930, it was named the ninth planet in our solar system. But in the years since, astronomers argued about it. Is Pluto truly a planet? After all, it is smaller than other planets. It has an unusual tilt. It travels in an odd orbit. Finally, in 2006, scientists met in Prague, Czech Republic. The International Astronomical Union voted on what is and what is not a planet. The final answer: Pluto is not a planet!

Pluto with Charon and two smaller moons ▼

Pluto has always been an oddball among planets. It has a weird, stretched-out orbit. It is very far away from the Sun, making it very cold and very dark. Because it is so small and distant, it wasn't even discovered until 1930. Charles Tombaugh, who discovered it, named it after the Roman god of the underworld.

NASA, ESA, H. Weaver (JHU/APL), A. Stern (SwRI) and the HST Pluto Companion Search Team

In 1975 a tiny moon, later named Charon, was spotted orbiting Pluto. In 2005 two more moons were discovered.

In the end the astronomers decided that only Mercury, Venus, Earth, Mars, Jupiter, Saturn, Uranus, and Neptune are "classical planets." They are celestial bodies in orbit around the Sun. Also, they are massive enough that they are nearly round. Each one has its own orbit. Pluto fails to make the grade because its orbit overlaps Neptune's path. Pluto is now classified as a dwarf planet.

All is not lost for Pluto, though. In January 2006, NASA launched the New Horizons spacecraft to study Pluto and its neighbors. Planet hunters are excited by what may be found beyond Pluto.

Richard Binzel, a professor at Massachusetts Institute of Technology, agrees: "Many more Plutos wait to be discovered."

Dan Durda/NASA-JPL

▲ An artist's drawing showing New Horizons approaching Pluto, with Charon in the background

Pluto vs. Earth

How is Pluto different from Earth? Find out with this chart.

	Pluto	Earth
surface	mostly covered by frozen nitrogen and rock	mostly covered by water (70%) and land
diameter	about 1,400 miles	about 8,000 miles
number of moons	3	1
average distance from the Sun	3.5 billion miles	93 million miles
orbit	It takes 248 Earth years to travel around the Sun.	It takes 365 days to travel around the Sun.
length of one day	about 154 hours	24 hours

Description Writing Frame

Use the Writing Frame below to orally summarize "The Moon's Shape."

There is much **interesting information** about the Moon.

For example, _____

_____ .

And the Moon's shape _____

_____ .

The Moon **moves** _____

_____ .

The Moon **also** orbits _____

_____ .

This is why the Moon's shape seems to change. As _____

_____ ,

we see different parts of it lighted.

In the four-week cycle of changing phases, we see, **for example,**

_____ .

Use the frame to write the summary on another sheet of paper.
Be sure to include the **bold** signal words. Keep this as a model
of this Text Structure.

Critical Thinking

1 The four-week cycle of changing phases is called the
   _____.

   A. lunar cycle

   B. Moon walk

   C. lighted half

2 Point to the sentences in "Eight Is Enough" that give facts about Pluto.

3 Find the chart in "Eight Is Enough." How are Pluto and Earth different?

4 Discuss the diagram on pages 84 and 85 with a partner. Talk about why the Moon appears to change shape.

> A diagram is a drawing or a plan. It explains the parts of something or the way it works.

Digital Learning

For a list of links and activities that relate to this Science standard, visit the California Treasures Web site at www.macmillanmh.com to access the Content Reader resources.

Have children view the Science e-Review "The Moon."

EL In addition, distribute copies of the Translated Concept Summaries in Spanish, Chinese, Hmong, Khmer, and Vietnamese.

The Sun and the Earth

Each day the Sun seems to move across the sky in a giant arc. In the morning the Sun appears low on the eastern horizon (huh•RIGH•zuhn), an imaginary line where the land seems to meet the sky. At midday, it appears high overhead. In the evening, it appears close to the western **horizon**. This is because Earth spins like a giant top. As Earth turns, one side faces the Sun. That side of Earth has daytime. The side that faces away from the Sun has nighttime.

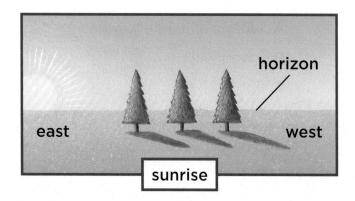

horizon

east — west

sunrise

east — west

midday

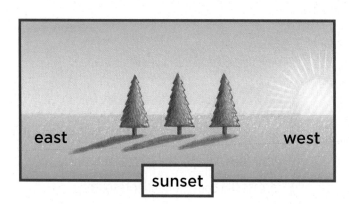

east — west

sunset

Seasons change as the Earth rotates around its axis and **revolves** (ri•VOLVZ) in a regular path around the Sun. An object that moves around another object revolves. Seasons change because Earth is tilted on its axis. No matter where Earth is in its orbit, its axis is always tilted in the same direction.

The Sun's position in the sky also seems to change from season to season. When it is summer in California, the Sun is high overhead at noon. That is because the northern half of Earth is tilted toward the Sun. This tilt makes the Sun's path seem higher in the sky.

When it is winter in California, the path of the Sun appears low in the sky. California is tilted away from the Sun. The Sun at noon is lower. The southern half of Earth is tilted toward the Sun.

Earth Revolves Around the Sun

spring

winter

summer

fall

LOOK!
UP IN THE SKY!

A solar eclipse leaves some people on Earth in the shadow of the Moon.

A total solar eclipse happens when the orbits of the Sun, the Moon, and Earth line up exactly. The Moon passes in front of the Sun and blocks it out while the shadow of the Moon travels across Earth. It's as if night has suddenly fallen. Then, just as suddenly, the Sun reappears. The area on Earth in the Moon's shadow is called the totality. Being in one can be an amazing experience.

What Happened to the Sun?
A total eclipse is possible because of a coincidence. The Moon and the Sun look about the same size in the sky. That's in spite of the fact that the Sun is really much bigger than the Moon. In fact, about 400 Moons could line up side by side across the Sun.

In a total solar eclipse, the Moon blocks the Sun's light. ▶

So how can the two objects appear to be the same size? The answer is that the Sun is about 400 times farther away than the Moon.

Because the Sun is 400 times bigger than the Moon and 400 times farther away, the two objects appear to be the same size! That means that when the Moon and Sun line up together, the Moon is just big enough to block out the Sun.

During an eclipse, the round disk of the Moon appears as a black circle over the Sun. Slowly the circle of the Moon moves across the Sun until it blocks it out completely. It keeps moving until the Sun begins to appear on the other side. It takes about three hours from start to finish. But the time of total darkness is just a few minutes. —*Andrea Delbanco*

Viewing Eclipses Safely

Looking at the Sun can seriously damage your eyes. That's why it's so important to be safe when viewing an eclipse. Here are some tips.

* Never look directly at the Sun with your naked eye, especially with a telescope or binoculars.

* The best way to view an eclipse is with a pinhole camera. Make one by putting a small hole in a piece of cardboard. Tilt the cardboard until the Sun shines through the hole. Put a piece of white paper or cardboard behind the hole so that the Sun hits it. Look at the white paper, and you will see a safe, clear picture of the solar eclipse. You'll also see sunspots!

This drawing shows how the Moon can block the Sun's light. ▼

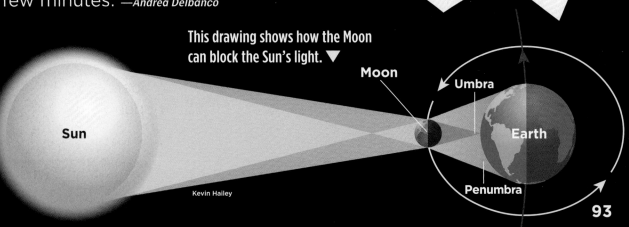

Sun

Moon

Umbra

Earth

Penumbra

Kevin Hailey

Compare/Contrast Writing Frame

**Use the Writing Frame below to orally summarize
"The Sun and the Earth."**

The Sun and the Earth are **both** _____.

The Sun seems to move across the sky, **however** _____

_____.

When one side of the Earth faces the Sun, this side of the Earth

_____.

In contrast, the side _____.

The Sun's position in the sky seems to change from season to

season. **However**, seasons _____.

When it is summer in California, the Sun _____.

The Sun's path seems higher, **however** _____

_____.

The Sun and Earth seem **similar** in that _____.

But the Sun and Earth are **different** because _____.

Use the frame to write the summary on another sheet of paper.
Be sure to include the **bold** signal words. Keep this as a model
of this Text Structure.

Critical Thinking

1 An object that moves around another object
_____.

    A. revolves

    B. rotates

    C. returns

2 Point out the sentence in "Look! Up in the Sky!" that tells what a total eclipse is.

3 Show a partner where the text in "Look! Up in the Sky!" tells how to view eclipses safely.

4 With a partner, compare the diagrams on pages 90 and 91.

> A diagram is a drawing or a plan. It explains the parts of something or the way it works.

Digital Learning

For a list of links and activities that relate to this Science standard, visit the California Treasures Web site at www.macmillanmh.com to access the Content Reader resources.

Have children view the Science in Motion video "Earth Revolves Around the Sun."

EL In addition, distribute copies of the Translated Concept Summaries in Spanish, Chinese, Hmong, Khmer, and Vietnamese.

DIFFERENT KINDS OF LAND

From snow-topped mountains to hot, dry deserts, California has it all! It has many kinds of land and water. It has high mountains and low, flat land. It has lakes and long rivers too.

The many hills and mountains of California are two kinds of landforms. Landforms are the shapes on the surface of Earth. California also has plains, which are large areas of flat or almost flat land.

▲ Some places in California are deserts.

California has valleys too. A valley is low land between hills or mountains. Valleys often have rivers flowing through them. A large valley called the Central Valley runs down the middle of California.

In addition, California has lakes, rivers, and streams. It is next to an ocean. These are called bodies of water. Salt water is found in oceans. Fresh water is found in lakes, rivers, ponds and streams.

California has many miles of coastline.

The study of land and water and the way people, plants, and animals live on and in them is called **geography**. Geography is important because it affects the way people live. Geographers, or people who study geography, divide California into eight **regions**. A region is an area with common features that set it apart from other areas. Kinds of landforms, bodies of water, and climate all shape a region. For example, the Sierra Nevada region is known for its snow-capped mountains.

Landforms, climate, and bodies of water affect how people live. Because these things are different from region to region, the way people live varies from region to region. Look at the "California Regions" map. Think about where you live. Is it flat or hilly? Is it near the ocean? Is it in a valley? What landforms does your region have? Are there bodies of water?

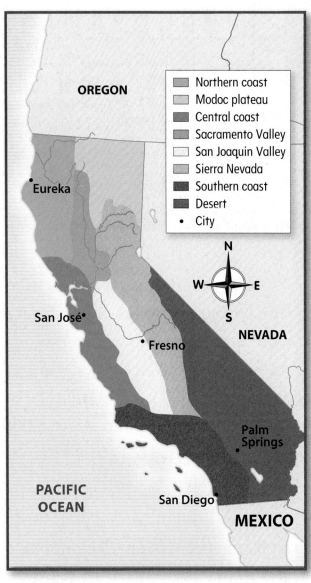

▲ On this map, each region is shown in a different color.

California Ecosystems

California offers a rich variety of habitats for humans and other living things.

More people mean more houses

California is huge. It covers 160,000 square miles. It has deserts and mountains, seacoasts and valleys. Its many ecosystems are home to 30,000 kinds of insects, 563 kinds of birds, and about 8,000 kinds of plants. That's more than in any other state.

Every kind of animal does best in its own ecosystem. Jackrabbits live in the desert. Seals live in the ocean. Elk and deer live in the grasslands. To protect the animals of California, people must protect the animals' ecosystems.

California is home to almost 40 million people. That number keeps growing. As more people come, they build more houses and roads. Animals are pushed aside.

To make sure that animals have a place to live, the state is passing laws to protect the land.

The California Desert

A lot of California is desert. Deserts are usually dry and hot. They have an amazing collection of plants and animals. Saguaro cactus, bighorn sheep, sidewinder snakes, desert tortoises, jackrabbits, and roadrunners all live in the deserts of California.

These deserts are in valleys and in highlands. Some of the most famous California deserts are the Mojave National Preserve, Death Valley, and Joshua Tree National Park.

In California, the deserts are formed in different ways. Some are the result of volcanoes and earthquakes. Others were once ancient seas.

Redwood Forests

Northern California has some of the biggest, oldest trees in the world. California redwoods can live for more than 2,000 years and grow to more than 369 feet tall. They live only where the air and land are wet and cool. The redwood forests are near the Pacific Ocean. In the summer, they get fog. In the winter, they get storms.

The animals that live in these forests like cool, moist weather. They include bears, pine martens, and many types of birds. There are also giant salamanders, red-bellied newts, silver salmon, and steelhead trout. Like many of California's ecosystems, the redwood forests are in danger. They are threatened by logging and pollution. Some areas of the forests are protected by law. Other are not. —*Lisa Jo Rudy*

Redwood Forest

Redwood Forest

Death Valley

Mojave National Preserve

Joshua Tree National Park

Key

Redwood Forest

Desert

Map Resources/Punchstock

California redwoods

Creatas/Punchstock

Description Writing Frame

Use the Writing Frame below to orally summarize "Different Kinds of Land."

California has **many interesting** kinds of land and water.

For example, _____

_____ .

Earth has shapes on its surface. **For example**, California has

_____

which are _____ .

California also has _____ ,

which are _____ .

For example, _____

_____ .

California has bodies of water. One example of these bodies of

water is _____ .

Other **examples** include _____ .

Use the frame to write the summary on another sheet of paper.
Be sure to include the **bold** signal words. Keep this as a model
of this Text Structure.

Critical Thinking

1   The study of land and water and the way people, plants, and animals live on them is called _____.

   A. climate

   B. landforms

   C. geography

2   Point out the sentences in "California Ecosystems" that describe California's deserts.

3   Show a partner the sentences in "California Ecosystems" that tell about California redwoods.

4   Use the map on page 97 to discuss the different regions of California with a partner.

> A map is a drawing that shows where different places are.

Digital Learning

For a list of links and activities that relate to this History/Social Science standard, visit the California Treasures Web site at www.macmillanmh.com to access the Content Reader resources. Have children view the video "Communities and Geography."

CHANGING THE LAND AND THE WATER

People adapt to the environment. They also change the environment to meet their needs. One way people change the environment is by building **dams.** A dam is a wall across a river or stream that holds back and controls the water. Dams let people store water for when they need it. In Northern California, for example, people built a dam across the Sacramento River. The water backed up and formed Shasta Lake. Now water from Shasta Lake can be sent south to the Sacramento Valley when it is needed.

Los Angeles was once a small town that got its water from the Los Angeles River. As the town grew into a city, it needed more water. So, the people in charge of the city's water system bought the rights to the land and water of the Owens River Valley. They built an **aqueduct** [AK wuh duct] to bring water from the Owens River to Los Angeles. An aqueduct is a long, human-made pipe for moving water from one place to another.

The Los Angeles aqueduct was built through mountains and across deserts. The workers dug tunnels through the mountains, made new roads, and built railroad tracks to carry supplies. They built power lines and telephone lines. All these things changed the environment.

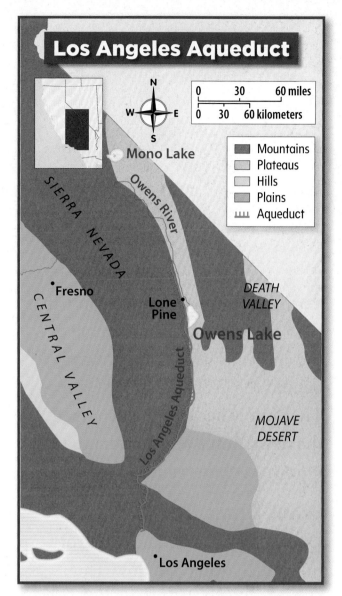

Los Angeles Aqueduct

| 0 | 30 | 60 miles |
| 0 | 30 | 60 kilometers |

Mono Lake

Owens River

SIERRA NEVADA

CENTRAL VALLEY

• Fresno

Lone Pine •

DEATH VALLEY

Owens Lake

Los Angeles Aqueduct

MOJAVE DESERT

• Los Angeles

Legend:
- Mountains
- Plateaus
- Hills
- Plains
- Aqueduct

▲ The Los Angeles Aqueduct changed the environment of California.

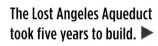
The Lost Angeles Aqueduct took five years to build. ▶

Barrie Rokeach

Deciding a Dam's Future

To keep the dam or not to keep the dam—that is a question many people in California disagree on.

Do you know where your water comes from? Many people in the San Francisco Bay Area know the answer. Theirs comes from behind the O'Shaughnessy Dam. They know because the dam is in the news. Some people want to take it down. Others want to keep it.

What Dams Do

Dams block rivers. They control how much water can flow. The water behind a dam rises. It floods the land there. The water is stored behind the dam until it is needed. Water controlled by dams is used to make electric power. It can also be used for drinking water or irrigation.

The Lost Valley

The O'Shaughnessy Dam is located inside the western edge of Yosemite National Park.

The dam was built in 1913 on the Tuolumne River. Water behind the dam flooded the Hetch Hetchy Valley. Like Yosemite Valley, the Hetch Hetchy was beautiful. Visitors came to see its huge waterfalls and towering cliffs. Artists painted its dramatic views. Now the valley's natural wonders are underwater.

Mount Holyoke College Art Museum

A painting of the Hetch Hetchy Valley before it was flooded

Debating the Dam: Keep It! Tear It Down!

A group called Restore Hetch Hetchy wants to take down the O'Shaughnessy Dam. Without the dam, the Tuolumne would flow freely again. People could see the beautiful valley.

Other people say that the dam is needed. It provides water and electricity to 2.4 million people and thousands of businesses. The costs of finding other sources of water and electricity are too high.

Dams: Answers and Questions

For years dams seemed like answers to important problems. They provided water and power.

Barrie Rokeach

▲ The O'Shaughnessey Dam (lower right) holds back the Tuolumne River.

The price seemed worth it. Now instead of answers, dams raise questions. Why can't rivers run free so fish can reproduce? Why can't beautiful natural wonders be uncovered?

Doing away with dams raises questions too. Where will water and power come from now?

The debate about dams will go on for a long time. What will the answer be for the O'Shaughnessy Dam? —*Susan Moger*

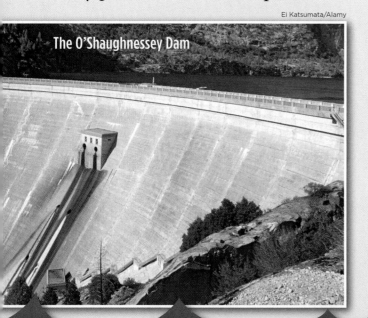

Ei Katsumata/Alamy

The O'Shaughnessey Dam

Problem/Solution Writing Frame

**Use the Writing Frame below to orally summarize
"Changing Land and Water."**

People change the environment to meet their needs. When

people need to **solve** a water **problem**, they might _____

_____.

Los Angeles was once a small town that had a **problem** when

_____.

The people in charge of the city's water system **solved** this

problem by _____

_____.

But then there was a new **problem**. The Los Angeles aqueduct

_____.

So, the workers _____

_____.

Use the frame to write the summary on another sheet of paper.
Be sure to include the **bold** signal words. Keep this as a model
of this Text Structure.

Critical Thinking

1. A long, human-made pipe for moving water is called an _____.

    A. railroad

    B. aqueduct

    C. aquarium

2. Point out the sentences in "Deciding a Dam's Future" that explain what dams do.

3. Read aloud the text in "Deciding a Dam's Future" that tells where the O'Shaughnessy Dam is located.

4. Use your finger to trace the Los Angeles aqueduct on the map on page 103.

A map is a drawing that shows where different places are.

Digital Learning

For a list of links and activities that relate to this History/Social Science standard, visit the California Treasures Web site at www.macmillanmh.com to access the Content Reader resources. Have children explore "Your Community's Land and Resources."

THE FIRST CALIFORNIANS

Native Americans were the first people to live in what is now California. They lived in different groups, each with its own **culture**. Culture is the way of life a group of people shares. Culture includes language, food, arts, and beliefs.

The Miwok [MEE Wahk] Native Americans lived in the Central Valley. Oak trees there provided acorns, which were important in the Miwok culture.

The Miwok had songs about acorns and used them to make bread. Each year the Miwok held a festival to celebrate the importance of acorns. Miwok people still hold this festival today.

The Chumash Native Americans lived in large villages along the southern coast. They got much of their food from the ocean, so boat building was important to them. They built large canoes for fishing.

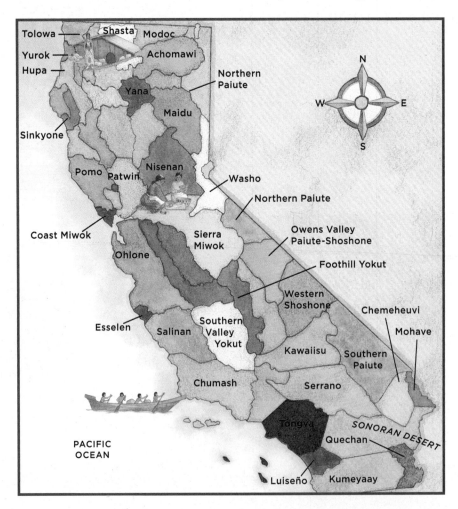

The Kawaiisu (kwigh EE soo) Native Americans moved from place to place as the seasons changed. In the winter they lived in sunny valleys of the Mojave (mo HAH vay) Desert. They built waterproof shelters of branches and bark. They warmed their homes using heated rocks. In the summer they moved up into the cool Tehachapi (tuh HA chuh pee) Mountains. Girls and women gathered berries, nuts, and acorns to eat. Boys and men hunted deer. The Kawaiisu also painted designs on rocks and rock walls. They made **petroglyphs** (PET roh glifs), or rock carvings.

▲ This headdress, made by the Hupa people, was used on special occasions.

The Hupa Native Americans lived along the Trinity River. They gathered berries and nuts to eat. They hunted deer and elk and made nets to catch fish in the river. The Hupa built strong houses from cedarwood and lived in villages close to the river.

Hupa dancers in the Jump Dance ▶

CELEBRATING AMERICAN INDIAN HERITAGE

November is National American Indian and Alaska Native Heritage Month.

A powwow in Indio, California

During November, Americans celebrate National American Indian and Alaska Native Heritage Month. During this month, we think about the culture and history of American Indians (also known as Native Americans) and Alaska Natives.

Honoring Heritage

The celebration of American Indian heritage started in 1916. At that time Americans celebrated for only one day. Each year in May, the nation would observe American Indian Day. In 1990, President George H. W. Bush signed the first proclamation that declared November as National American Indian Heritage Month.

In 2004 the federal government focused more attention on Native Americans when it opened the National Museum of the American Indian in Washington, D.C. This Smithsonian museum honors the history, arts, and lives of Native Americans.

AP Photo/Lawrence Jackson

The National Museum of the American Indian opened in 2004. The Eskimo mask below is on display there.

The Granger Collection, New York

American Indian and Alaska Native History

Native Americans and Alaska Natives lived in what is now North and South America for thousands of years before explorers arrived in the 1400s. When Christopher Columbus reached the islands off southeastern North America in 1492, he called the people he met Indians. That's because he wrongly thought he had sailed to India.

Before Europeans arrived, there were between 12 million and 15 million American Indians and Alaska Natives. After Europeans began to colonize the land, disease and war killed hundreds of thousands of American Indians.

Today, American Indians and Alaska Natives make up about 1.5 percent of the U.S. population, or about 4.1 million people. California is home to more than 100 American Indian tribes. There, people of American Indian heritage make up about 1.2 percent of the population. That's about 440,000 people. —*Jill Egan*

Frank and Frances Carpenter collection/ Library of Congress

▲ An Eskimo man and his child

Did you know?

There are more than 550 federally recognized American Indian groups in the United States.

The largest Alaska Native group is the Tlingit, with about 17,200 people.

538,000 American Indians and Alaska Natives live on reservations.

Cause/Effect Writing Frame

**Use the Writing Frame below to orally summarize
"The First Californians."**

Native Americans were the first people to live in what we now
call California. **Because** the Miwok Native Americans lived in the

Central Valley, with oak trees, _____ .

As a result, _____ .

The **effect** of this today is that _____

_____ .

Because they wanted to keep warm in the winter, the Kawaiisu _____

_____ .

Because they wanted to keep cool in the summer, they _____

_____ .

For the Hupa Native Americans, the **effect** of living along a river

was that _____ .

Use the frame to write the summary on another sheet of paper.
Be sure to include the **bold** signal words. Keep this as a model
of this Text Structure.

Critical Thinking

1. A way of life that a people shares is called a _____.

   A. culture

   B. Chumash

   C. petroglyph

2. Find the sentence in "Celebrating American Indian Heritage" that tells what Americans celebrate during the month of November.

3. Revisit the text of "Celebrating American Indian Heritage" to reread why Christopher Columbus called the people he met Indians.

4. Talk about the different California Native American groups with a partner. Use the map on page 108 to guide you.

A map is a drawing that shows where different places are.

Digital Learning

For a list of links and activities that relate to this History/Social Science standard, visit the California Treasures Web site at www.macmillanmh.com to access the Content Reader resources. Have children view the video "Native American Communities."

CALIFORNIA COMMUNITIES

LIFE IN A KUMEYAAY VILLAGE

The Kumeyaay [KOO mee yigh] have lived in Southern California for thousands of years. The climate of this area made it an ideal place to live. The environment provided food, water, shelter, and even medicine.

The Kumeyaay hunted with bows and arrows made from willow branches and deer **ligaments,** which are strong bands of stretchy tissue that connect bones. To hunt large animals such as deer and bighorn sheep, the hunters used arrows with stone arrowheads. Women sometimes used **snares,** or traps, to catch small animals such as rabbits, or hunted them with wooden arrowheads. Animals provided food, and their skins provided clothing, blankets, and rugs.

▲ Kumeyaay bows were made from willow branches.

◀ The Kumeyaay used the agave (ah GAH vay) plant to treat cuts and infections.

Like the Kawaiisu, the Kumeyaay moved throughout the year, hunting and gathering food. In the winter, many lived on the coast. They fished and gathered clams. Their winter houses were huts made of willow branches with the leaves left on them. Each house had a small door, which was covered with a mat or basket at night to keep out the cold air.

During the summer the Kumeyaay moved into the mountains. Summer shelters were simple, might even be caves. In the summer these American Indians gathered wild plums and other fruits.

In the fall they gathered nuts and acorns. The Kumeyaay collected as many nuts and acorns as they could to eat over the winter.

Kumeyaay Lands, About 1770

Escondido Creek

San Diego River

San Diego

Tijuana River

Colorado River

PACIFIC OCEAN

Sea of Cortez

0   25   50 miles
0   25   50 kilometers

Kumeyaay lands
Present-day boundaries

N
W E
S

The Kumeyaay used baskets like this to gather acorns. ▶

MANY TRIBES, MANY CULTURES

Depending on where they lived, American Indian groups in California had different ways of life.

Many groups of American Indians have lived in California for thousands of years. Some tribes lived in the forests, near lakes and rivers. They built villages, hunted, and fished.

Still other Indian tribes lived near the sea. They built strong canoes, fished in the sea, and hunted for other seafood.

Desert Indians had to search for food and water. They became skilled hunters and gatherers. When food in one place became scarce, they traveled to a new place.

The Chumash Indians of the Sea

The Chumash people lived in what is now Southern California. They lived in big and small villages along the Pacific Coast.

Butler Institute of American Art/The Bridgeman Art Library

▲ An American Indian camp in what is now Yosemite National Park

◄ A reconstructed Chumash house

Jupiter Images/Brand X/Alamy

They got food from the sea. Their wooden seagoing canoes were called *tomols*. A tomol could be 30 feet long and big enough to hold 12 people.

Most Chumash lived in houses of woven bulrushes and cattails. Some lived in houses made of whale bones. The Chumash used shells for money. When it was warm, they wore little clothing. When it was cold, they dressed in animal skins.

Today the Chumash tribe is still active. There are many Californians who are all or part Chumash Indian.

◄ Chumash basket

Bildarchiv Preussischer Kulturbesitz/Art Resource

The Serrano People of Central California

The Serrano Indians lived in Big Bear Valley in Central California. They lived near springs, streams, and rivers. Serrano women made beautiful pottery. The Serrano people ate vegetables such as nuts, berries, herbs, and roots. They hunted rabbits, birds, and other animals. They wore clothing made of deerskin.

Edward S. Curtis/Library of Congress

1924 photograph of a Serrano woman

Serrano people built small villages of about 10 to 30 homes. To build their homes, they dug circles and then built frames of poles. The poles were covered with brush. —*Lisa Jo Rudy*

Edward S. Curtis/Library of Congress

Serrano man, 1924

Description Writing Frame

Use the Writing Frame below to orally summarize "Life in a Kumeyaay Village."

The Kumeyaay have lived in Southern California because the

environment provided **features such as** _____

_____ .

The Kumeyaay hunted with tools made from the environment.

For instance, bows and arrows _____

_____ .

Arrowheads were made from materials **that included**

_____ .

The animals of Southern California were **important** to the Kumeyaay

because _____ .

In the winter the Kumeyaay lived on the coast. There the

environment provided food **such as** _____ .

Use the frame to write the summary on another sheet of paper.
Be sure to include the **bold** signal words. Keep this as a model
of this Text Structure.

Critical Thinking

1. Strong bands of stretchy tissue that connect bones are called _____.

   A. ligaments

   B. leaves

   C. blankets

2. Point to the sentence in "Many Tribes, Many Cultures" that tells where the Chumash people lived.

3. Read aloud the text from "Many Tribes, Many Cultures" that tells what Serrano women made.

4. Use the map on page 115 to tell a partner about the Kumeyaay lands in California.

A map is a drawing that shows where different places are.

Digital Learning

For a list of links and activities that relate to this History/Social Science standard, visit the California Treasures Web site at www.macmillanmh.com to access the Content Reader resources. Have children visit "A Native American Child in California."

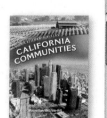

LEADING THE KUMEYAAY

The Kumeyaay people lived in small groups called bands. Each band had its own land and used the natural resources on it. Because the Kumeyaay had so many people and covered such a large territory, they worked out a plan for **government**. A government is a group of people in charge of leading a community, a state, or a nation.

Much of the Kumeyaay homeland was desert.

▼ A Kumeyaay leader wearing a ceremonial headdress.

The Kumeyaay was divided into regions. Each region had a general who was in charge of the bands who lived there. A band could have as many as 1,000 people. Each band had a leader called a Captain. Each captain had a **council** [KOWN suhl]. A council is a group of people who work with a leader to make decisions. Each band had a central village where the leader and his council lived. Important **ceremonies** were held here. A ceremony is a special way of doing something to mark an important time.

The **shaman** was an important member of the council. A shaman was a religious leader who lead the shaman ceremonies. The Kumeyaay believed being a shaman was something a child was "called to." If a child had this special calling, he or she was taught prayers, songs, and knowledge. The council also included healers who used medicines from plants and herbs, as well as special songs.

▲ Plumes of eagle feathers were used for some Kumeyaay ceremonies.

The Kumeyaay celebrated important events with special ceremonies. The shaman would study the stars and decide the best time to hold a ceremony. There were ceremonies to celebrate when girls became women and boys became men, marriages, when babies were named, and to honor the dead. Ceremonies often involved singing, dancing, drumming, and storytelling. The Kumeyaay also used songs and dances to pray for good hunting and for the health of the people.

Five Kumeyaay elders leading a ceremony. ▶

The
KARUK INDIAN TRIBE
OF NORTHERN CALIFORNIA

The Karuk (Karok) people of northern California
have a rich tradition of protecting the land.

▲ Mount Shasta

The History of the Karuk Tribe

American Indians have lived in California for thousands of years. The Karuk (Karok) Tribe had about 1,200 members when Europeans arrived in the 1700s. They lived in the Klamath River valley near Mount Shasta. Their land was filled with mountains and fresh water.

California's rich northern rain forest was a good place to hunt and fish. The Karuk (Karok), like many other tribes, had villages among the rivers, lagoons, and bays. They used dugout canoes to travel up and down the Klamath River. The canoes were made of redwood trees.

◄ A 1924 photograph of a Karuk woman

Tribal elders were in charge of the tribe. They decided who could fish and hunt on their land. The Karuk (Karok) also owned slaves, who were from conquered tribes.

Mount Shasta, in northern California, was sacred to the Karuk (Karok). They held the World Renewal Ceremony there.

The World Renewal Ceremony was held in the fall. The people prepared by cleansing in the rivers. They danced and prayed to the spirits. The World Renewal Ceremony was a very important event to prevent earthquakes, floods, and crop failures.

The Karuk Tribe Now

Today, the Karuk (Karok) tribe still lives near Mount Shasta. They have changed, but in many ways they are still the same. They still hunt and fish. They still make beautiful baskets and other artwork. They still celebrate World Renewal at Mount Shasta.

Most important, the Karuk (Karok) people are still protectors of the land. They work to keep Mount Shasta and the Klamath River clean. For many years, the United States government fought with the Karuk (Karok). The Karuk (Karok) people were forced to live in a small reservation. They did not have the same rights as most Americans.

Today, though, the Karuk (Karok) are working together with the U.S. Forest Service to protect the land. The Forest Service is learning about land management from the Karuk (Karok). —*Lisa Jo Rudy*

▼ A 2007 photograph of a Karuk woman and her child

Cause/Effect Writing Frame

**Use the Writing Frame below to orally summarize
"Leading the Kumeyaay."**

Because the Kumeyaay had so many people and covered such a

large territory, _____ .

The **effect** of this was that each region had people in charge

known as _____ .

The Kumeyaay also had councils or groups of people who _____

_____ .

A shaman was an important member of a council **because** _____

_____ .

If a child had a special calling to become a shaman, **then** _____

_____ .

Because the Kumeyaay celebrated important events with special

ceremonies, _____ .

Use the frame to write the summary on another sheet of paper.
Be sure to include the **bold** signal words. Keep this as a model
of this Text Structure.

Critical Thinking

1 A group of people in charge of leading a community, a state, or a nation is called a _____.

   A. shaman

   B. gathering

   C. government

2 Point to the sentences in "The Karuk Indian Tribe of Northern California" that tell you about the canoes of the Karuk (Karok).

3 Work with a partner to find information about the World Renewal Ceremony in "The Karuk Indian Tribe of Northern California."

4 Read aloud the caption for the photograph of the Kumeyaay leader on page 120. What does the caption tell you about the photograph?

A caption is a title or an explanation of a photograph.

Digital Learning

For a list of links and activities that relate to this History/Social Studies standard, visit the California Treasures Web site at www.macmillanmh.com to access the Content Reader resources. Have children watch the video "Native American Communities."

NEWCOMERS BRING CHANGE

For thousands of years the Kawaiisu, the Hupa, the Kumeyaay, and other Native American groups lived in California. In 1492 Christopher Columbus sailed to North America. About 50 years later, Spanish **explorers** sailed up what is now the California coast. Explorers are people who go to a place that is new to them to find out about it.

Once Spanish settlers came to stay, life began to change for California Native Americans. The newcomers took the land. Native Americans fought back, but the newcomers had better weapons. The new people also brought diseases. California's Native Americans had never had diseases such as smallpox or measles. Many became sick and died.

▲ A Spanish soldier on or about the year 1790

▼ Some Kumeyaay Native Americans were forced to live and work at Spanish settlements.

By the early 1900s most Native American groups had lost their homelands. Some lived on **reservations**. A reservation is land set aside for Native Americans by the United States government. However, in California, most Native American groups were not given reservations.

▲ A Hupa woman making a basket

The Hupa were able to hold on to much of their original homeland. But instead of living only by hunting and fishing, many began to farm. Today the Hupa earn money through logging and selling wood from their forest homeland.

When the Spanish settled on Kumeyaay lands on the coast, the Native Americans were forced to leave their winter homes and stay in the mountains all year. When California became part of the United States, more and more settlers came to the state. The Kumeyaay lost more land. They lost their rights and were treated unfairly.

Hupa logging on their reservation ▶

Welcome to the
National Museum
OF THE
American
INDIAN

This museum honors the history
and cultures of Native Americans.

Michael Ventura/Alamy

A new museum opened in Washington,
D.C., in 2004. It is the National Museum of the
American Indian. A member of the Blackfoot
tribe helped to design the museum. The
museum looks a little like a rock formation in
the desert of the American Southwest.

A Collector's Quest

Not everything in the museum was collected
by American Indians. Many of the objects in
the museum were collected by George Heye.
Heye was not a Native American.

George Heye was born in 1874. His father
made a lot of money by drilling oil on Indian
land. George became interested in Indian
people and customs. He started buying Indian
items when he was in college. For almost
60 years he bought every item he could from
different tribes. Finally he owned 800,000
Native American items. His tiny museum
couldn't hold them all!

▲ An American Indian neck
ornament made more than
1,000 years ago and found
in Tennessee

Werner Foreman/Topham/The Image Works

Werner Forman/Corbis Images

▲ A headdress made by Indians
of the Northwest Coast

Heye's collection is now a big part of the National Museum of the American Indian. Native American people run the museum. They decide what is shown in the galleries. They decide how their stories should be told.

The museum tells a story that goes back 10,000 years. It tells about Native American lives, beliefs, and people. Over time, each tribe will have a chance to tell its own story.

▲ Pomo Indians Chief Little John, 110 years old, and his great grandson Little Eagle Feather, 1933

The Pomo Indian People

The Pomo are Native Americans. Their story will be told in the museum, as will the stories of all Native American peoples.

The Pomo people lived all over California. They hunted, fished, and gathered fruits and nuts. The Pomo were peaceful people who lived a simple life.

When Russians came to California, the Pomo made friends with them. Later, though, the Pomo suffered from diseases like smallpox that they got from the Russians. Many Pomo were captured by raiders and forced into slavery.

Today the Pomo own only 50 acres of land in Northern California. There are, however, 75 Pomo tribes. All of the tribes are well known for their beautiful baskets and artwork. —*Lisa Jo Rudy*

▼ Pomo baskets

Sequence Writing Frame

Use the Writing Frame below to orally summarize "Newcomers Bring Change."

For thousands of years the Kawaiisu, the Hupa, the Kumeyaay, and other Native American groups lived in California. **Then,**

in 1492, _____

_____ .

About 50 years **later,** _____

_____ .

After Spanish settlers came to stay, _____

_____ .

After the Spanish settled on Kumeyaay lands on the coast, _____

_____ .

When California became part of the United States, _____

_____ .

Use the frame to write the summary on another sheet of paper. Be sure to include the **bold** signal words. Keep this as a model for writing a summary of this Text Structure.

Critical Thinking

1 People who go to a place that is new to them to find out about it are called _____.

    A. explorers

    B. groups

    C. nutrients

2 Revisit "Welcome to the National Museum of the American Indian." Why is George Heye's collection of Native American items important?

3 Point out three facts in "Welcome to the National Museum of the American Indian" about the Pomo Indian people.

4 Discuss with a partner how the photograph of the men logging on page 127 supports the text in "Newcomers Bring Change."

A photograph is a picture taken with a camera.

Digital Learning

For a list of links and activities that relate to this History/Social Science standard, visit the California Treasures Web site at www.macmillanmh.com to access the Content Reader resources. Have children watch the video "Native American Communities."

131

TOWNS WITH SPANISH BACKGROUND

How did your community begin? If your town is one of the many places in California whose name begins with *San* or *Santa*, then it may have been settled by the Spanish. Spanish explorers claimed California for Spain. The first person from Spain to see the area was Juan Rodriguez Cabrillo (kah BREE yoh). He was a sea captain exploring the California coast in 1542. Sixty years later another Spanish sea captain explored California's coast. His name was Sebastián Vizcaíno (viz cah EE no). When a terrible storm almost sank his ships, he sailed to safety into an area that he named Santa Barbara.

Spanish settlers built settlements and missions. A **mission** [MISH un] is a settlement built around a church. In 1786 Spanish settlers founded Mission Santa Barbara. Today you can find many places in California with a Spanish **heritage**. Heritage means something handed down from the past.

Explorers and Founders

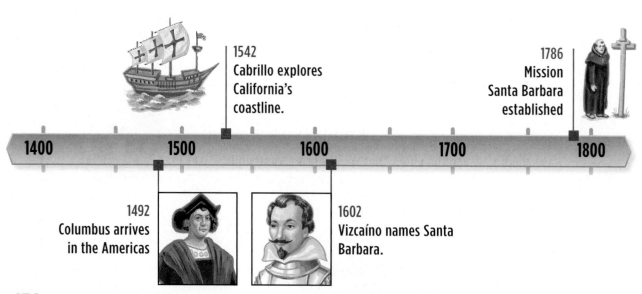

1542
Cabrillo explores California's coastline.

1786
Mission Santa Barbara established

1400   1500   1600   1700   1800

1492
Columbus arrives in the Americas

1602
Vizcaíno names Santa Barbara.

NEW PEOPLE, NEW TOWNS

After 1848 people rushed to California from all over the world to find gold. Mining camps and towns sprang up.

During the 1940s, many people began to **migrate**, or move, to California from other parts of the United States. Some people began to plan **developments**, or groups of houses. People bought houses as fast as workers could build them. Today new families from Latin America and Asia have moved into these developments, bringing their cultures.

Some families came to California from far away. Philip Choy's family came from China. As a boy, Philip went to a public school. But he also went to a special school to learn his Chinese culture. Today Philip Choy's grandchildren are learning the Chinese language and culture.

▲ Lakewood, California

▼ Philip Choy (from left), age six, with his family in 1932.

▼ The Choy family today

Legacy of Dreams

They didn't start out as Americans, but immigrants still go after the American dream.

David Frasier/Photo Edit

People come to the United States from around the world. They may not speak good English when they arrive. They may have little education. To make a living, some immigrants work picking fruit, sewing clothes, and doing other jobs that require few skills. Soon, though, many immigrants learn enough to start their own businesses.

▲ This immigrant woman earns a living by picking fruit.

Coming to America, Finding the American Dream

Often, people from India go into the hotel business. Some people from Korea make clothes or sell groceries. Many people from Mexico, who came to pick fruit, now own farms and vineyards. At first, these businesses are small, but they are big enough to make a living. Even the children work in the businesses. When those children grow up, many go off to college.

Spencer Grant/Photo Edit

This immigrant family owns a store. ▶

Coming Home to the Family Business

In the past, many of the children of immigrants had little interest in their families' business. But that trend seems to be changing. Instead of walking away from their parents' businesses, grown children of immigrants are coming back. They're taking a second look. Many are discovering they have good ideas to make their parents' businesses better.

Peter Kim and his father

Stephanie Diani

That's what happened with Peter Kim, a Korean American from southern California. He went back to help with his father's failing clothing business. With his new ideas, he turned the company into a big success.

Priti Patel's family came from India. At age 8, she was counting change and working the front desk. "I used to hate it," she says. "Everybody else gets to go home after school and get a snack. I had to help at the hotel. On weekends I had to cut grass." When friends drove by and saw her working, she would feel embarrassed. Later, though, Patel earned a business degree. She returned to her family business. Today she runs one of her family's motels.

Citizenship: the true American dream

AP Photo/Nick Ut

These Americans are finding a way to build on the American dreams their parents worked so hard for.

Sequence Writing Frame

Use the Writing Frame below to orally summarize "Towns with Spanish Background."

The **first** person from Spain to see California, in 1542, _____

_____ .

Sixty years **later** _____

_____ .

When a terrible storm almost sank his ships, _____

_____ .

Later, in 1786, Spanish settlers _____

_____ .

Today _____ .

After 1848 _____ .

Then, during the 1940s, _____

_____ .

Today _____ .

Use the frame to write the summary on another sheet of paper. Be sure to include the **bold** signal words. Keep this as a model of this Text Structure.

Critical Thinking

1 _____ means something handed down from the past.

    A. Mission

    B. House

    C. Heritage

2 Revisit the text of "Legacy of Dreams" and point out the sentences that tell what some people from different countries do to make a living in the United States.

3 Find the paragraph in "Legacy of Dreams" that tells about Priti Patel. Describe her situation to a partner.

4 Discuss the events of the time line on page 132 with a partner.

A time line is a line of significant events in a subject area.

Digital Learning

For a list of links and activities that relate to this History/Social Science standard, visit the California Treasures Web site at www.macmillanmh.com to access the Content Reader resources. Have children view the video "Communities Change."

A GOLD RUSH TOWN

When gold was discovered in California, people came hoping to get rich by finding some of it. Miners had **claims**. A claim is a legal right to mine on a certain area of land. Often there were no rules or police. Miners sometimes made up their own rules to protect their claims.

Although the miners came to California in search of gold, they still needed to eat. They needed their laundry cleaned, too. Instead of digging for gold, some people started businesses. They sold hardware or ran hotels or restaurants. During the Gold Rush, some people got rich from gold, but more people got rich by selling goods and services to miners.

▼ Gold miners visited barber shops to get shaves.

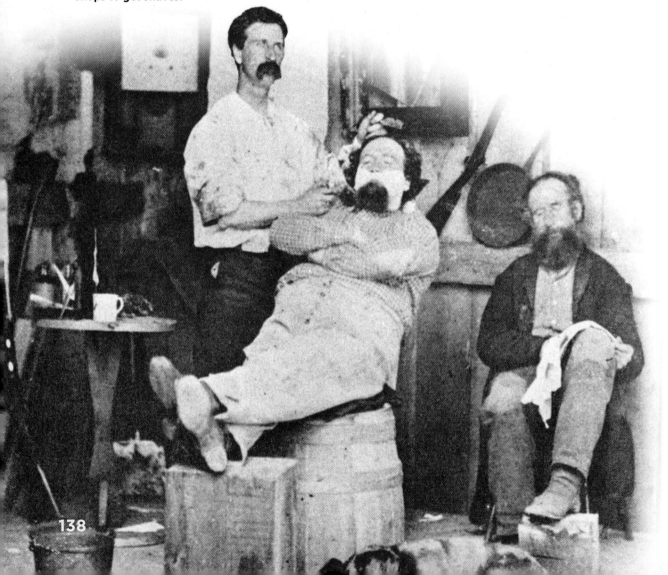

How was your community established? San Francisco, for example, grew from a tiny settlement into a large city. This began when ships carrying gold seekers arrived during the Gold Rush. After these people left the ships to find gold, some of the ships were sunk. Dirt and stones were added to the harbor to make **landfill**. Landfill is dry land that people have made by filling in watery areas. Today some of San Francisco stands on landfill.

How have people and families contributed to founding your community? Spanish settlers founded some towns and cities in California. During the Gold Rush, people from other countries such as China settled in gold-mining towns. They started businesses. Small towns grew and developed. Later, Vietnamese Americans came to California to escape a war in Vietnam. Seema Handu and her husband came from India. "We love that there are people here from many different countries."

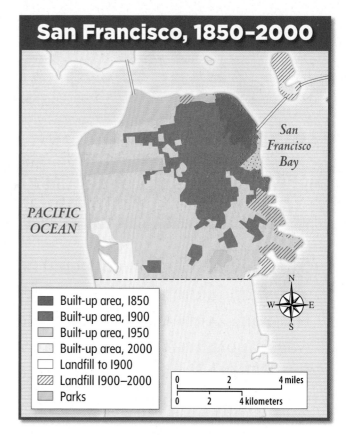

San Francisco, 1850–2000

■	Built-up area, 1850
■	Built-up area, 1900
▢	Built-up area, 1950
▢	Built-up area, 2000
▢	Landfill to 1900
▨	Landfill 1900–2000
▨	Parks

0   2   4 miles
0 2 4 kilometers

▲ How has San Francisco changed over time?

▼ Immigrants and their families help California towns and cities grow.

139

A Lifetime of Treasures

Mayme Clayton left a legacy of African American cultural riches.

courtesy Avery Clayton

▲ **Mayme Clayton**

Mayme Clayton collected books, magazines, and letters written by African Americans. Her son, Avery Clayton, thought her collection was important. The books were rare and hard to find. They were written by authors who helped shape African American culture.

One book in the collection was written by Phillis Wheatley. Wheatley was a slave who wrote poetry. She was the first African American to publish a book. Wheatley herself signed the book in the Claytons' collection. No one else owns a copy signed by Phillis Wheatley.

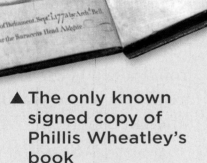
Melissa Roth/The New York Times/Redux

▲ **The only known signed copy of Phillis Wheatley's book**

By the time she died at age 83, Mrs. Clayton had more than 30,000 books by or about black people. Her collection also includes papers about slaves, photographs, movies, sheet music, and personal letters by black leaders and artists. It is one of the biggest private collections of African American history and culture in the United States.

Avery Clayton's dream was to create a museum for his mother's treasures. Scholars say that Mrs. Clayton's collection is extremely important. Without her work, part of African American heritage would have been lost. "We didn't know these things existed," says Sara Hodson of California's Huntington Library.

The collection's new home is likely to be in Culver City, California. Part of Avery Clayton's dream is to share the cultural riches his mother collected with others. He especially wants kids to have a chance to see the collection. "African American culture is currently being defined by pop culture," he says. "It's important to offer a more complete picture." —*Kathryn Satterfield*

▲ Avery Clayton with a poster from his mother's collection

◄ Books like these make Mrs. Clayton's collection extremely important.

courtesy Avery Clayton

Compare/Contrast Writing Frame

Use the Writing Frame below to orally summarize "A Gold Rush Town."

Each period of settlement in California was somewhat different.

When gold was discovered, miners had claims, or _____

_____ .

However, miners _____ .

During the rush for gold, some people got rich, **but** _____

_____ .

When gold seekers arrived in San Francisco, it was _____

_____ .

However, it _____ .

In the beginning, Spanish settlers in California _____

_____ .

But then, during the Gold Rush, _____ .

Unlike in the beginning, today _____ .

Use the frame to write the summary on another sheet of paper. Be sure to include the **bold** signal words. Keep this as a model of this Text Structure.

Critical Thinking

1 Dry land that people have made by filling in watery areas is

called _____.

    A. landfill

    B. laundry

    C. large city

2 Point out the sentences in "A Lifetime of Treaures" that explain what Mayme Clayton did.

3 Read aloud the text in this article that tells why Mrs. Clayton's collection is extremely important.

4 Describe for a partner the map on page 139. What does it show?

A map is a drawing that shows where different places are.

Digital Learning

For a list of links and activities that relate to this History/Social Science standard, visit the California Treasures Web site at www.macmillanmh.com to access the Content Reader resources. Have children view the video "Communities Change."

RULES AND LAWS PROTECT EVERYONE

Communities and countries need rules. When a rule is made by a government for people in a community it is called a **law**. Some laws help keep people safe, such as laws that tell drivers what speed is allowed. Other laws protect property. Laws say that no one may come into your home or take something of yours without your permission. People who break laws are punished. They may have to pay money or go to jail.

Our government has to follow rules, too. Some of the most important rules the government must follow are in the United States Constitution. A constitution is a plan for government. Our country's Constitution was written more than 200 years ago. It says what our government can and cannot do. The people we elect promise to obey the Constitution.

Rules and laws protect people. ▶

BEACH RULES
- NO SWIMMING BEYOND THE SWIM LINE. ALL SWIMMERS MUST STAY WITHIN THE DESIGNATED SWIM AREAS.
- ALCOHOLIC BEVERAGES ARE PROHIBITED.
- PLEASE DO NOT THROW STONES OR ROCKS.

▲ The United States Constitution begins with the words "We the People."

Following rules and laws is part of being a good citizen. Good citizens believe in the **common good**—doing what is best for everyone. Good citizens know that rules and laws protect everyone.

Have you ever helped out at your school or in your community? You are being a good citizen if you read to younger children at a school, help others in the classroom, pick up trash, or collect cans for a food drive.

Being involved in school government is another way to help your school community. You could even stay involved with government as you grow up. You could work to improve schools.

Voting is a responsibility of being a good citizen. When people vote, they make decisions about laws and the people they want in government.

Helping others is one way to be a good citizen. ▶

Teens to the Rescue!

These emergency medical service members are all well trained, certified, and in their teens.

Post 53 EMTs, left to right: Wells Landers, 18; Kate Kevorkian, 17; Annie Maybell, 17; Emily Stout, 17

Emily Stout's heart raced as she and her crewmates jumped out of their ambulance on I-95 in Darien, Connecticut. Slumped against a concrete barrier was a stunned-looking man. His leg was bloody. His crushed car lay just a few feet away.

Within minutes, Emily and the others placed the victim in a special collar to protect his neck. They bandaged his leg, and lifted him onto a stretcher and into the ambulance. Then they sped off to nearby Stamford Hospital. There they wheeled him into the emergency room.

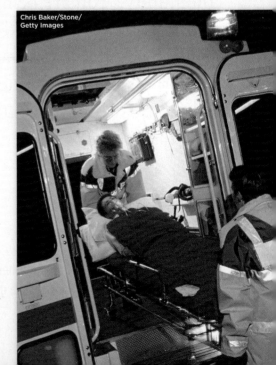

Chris Baker/Stone/ Getty Images

EMTs at work ▶

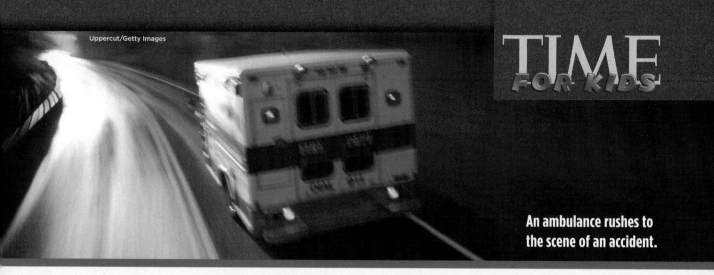

Uppercut/Getty Images

An ambulance rushes to the scene of an accident.

Emily and 58 other teen volunteers work for the Darien Emergency Medical Service. Their service is called Post 53. It is the only ambulance service in Darien.

With some help from trained adults, these teens take about 1,450 calls each year. They respond to car crashes and heart attacks and even help deliver babies. "They're superb," says Timothy S. Hall, Stamford Hospital's chairman of surgery. "I've had cases where patients wouldn't have lived without them."

Post 53 was started in 1969 as an Eagle Scout project. Teens who join the team must pass a screening, do 140 hours of training, and take an exam. At the end, they become certified emergency medical technicians.

They are on call 120 hours a month. They carry radio transmitters everywhere, even to class. They drop everything when they're called.

"Once, I had to leave three minutes before Harry Potter ended," Emily Stout says. All the work is worth it. Just ask Jim Cloud. When Cloud's heart stopped, the teens got it started again. Jim's wife says: "They saved his life. They're magnificent." —*Molly Lopez*

courtesy of Stamford Hospital

Dr. Timothy Hall says the teens have saved the lives of some of his patients. ▶

Description Writing Frame

**Use the Writing Frame below to orally summarize
"Rules and Laws Protect Everyone."**

Communities and countries need rules. Some laws, **for example**,

_____ .

Laws **such as** these include _____

_____ .

Our government has rules to follow too. Some of **the most**

important rules are in _____ .

Following rules and laws is part of being _____ .

Good citizens, **for instance**, _____

_____ .

To begin with, good citizens know _____

_____ .

Good citizens do things **such as** _____

_____ .

Use the frame to write the summary on another sheet of paper.
Be sure to include the **bold** signal words. Keep this as a model
of this Text Structure.

Critical Thinking

1 A rule that is made by a government for people in a community is called a _____.

    A. land

    B. plan

    C. law

2 Point to the sentences in "Teens to the Rescue!" that tell how some teens help others.

3 Read aloud the text that tells what teens have to do to join Post 53. Why would following rules be important to these teens?

4 Talk about the photograph of the Constitution and its caption on page 145 with a partner. What does the caption tell you about the photograph?

A caption is a title or an explanation of a photograph.

Digital Learning

For a list of links and activities that relate to this History/Social Science standard, visit the California Treasures Web site at www.macmillanmh.com to access the Content Reader resources. Have children view the video "Many Communities, One Nation."

SYMBOLS OF OUR COUNTRY

Did you know that the bald eagle is our national bird? Its strength and independence stands for the strength and freedom of the United States.

What do you think of when you see an American flag? The flag is a **symbol** of our country. A symbol is something that stands for something else. The stars of our flag stand for the 50 states. The stripes stand for the original 13 colonies.

The Statue of Liberty is another symbol. **Liberty** means freedom from control by someone else. For many it symbolizes our country's freedom.

The Declaration of Independence is the document that explained to the world why the United States wanted to be free and independent. We remember the ideas of freedom when we see it.

Symbols remind us of important ideas. ▼

Local Landmarks and Symbols

Communities have important symbols and landmarks, too. These symbols and landmarks tell us about the history of our communities. They also tell us what our communities think is important.

The city seal of Oakland, California, honors one of its landmarks, the large oak tree in front of City Hall. The oak tree is a symbol of strength. It also reminds people of Oakland's natural beauty and resources.

The word *Eureka* on the California seal reminds us of the discovery of gold.

Symbols remind us of important ideas.

▼ The oak tree is a symbol of Oakland.

Open Liberty!

A safer, more secure Statue of Liberty welcomes visitors.

Every year thousands of visitors to New York City come to see the Statue of Liberty. For more than 100 years, they were allowed to walk inside and climb the 354 steps to the crown.

All of that changed on September 11, 2001. After the terrorist attacks, the statue and its grounds on Liberty Island were closed to visitors. Officials worried that the site wasn't safe. The island reopened three months later, but the statue remained closed. Finally officials announced that visitors could enter the statue once again beginning in the summer of 2004.

Now, though, tourists can only climb to the top of the statue's pedestal.

A Towering Symbol

The Statue of Liberty came to the United States in 1885. It was a gift from the people of France. It recognized the friendship between the countries during the American Revolution.

The head of the Statue of Liberty in Paris, France, 1883 ▼

Around 1900

Archive Holdings Inc./Getty Images

Today

WizData, Inc./Alamy

The statue became a symbol of freedom and democracy. Immigrants saw it and knew they were safe and free. Before 9/11, nearly 6 million people toured Lady Liberty each year. After 9/11, the number of visitors fell by about 40 percent.

To get into the Statue of Liberty, visitors must call ahead. They must go through security systems. It's better than not getting in at all. U.S. Representative Anthony Weiner of New York says that the reopening is "great news." But he hopes tourists will one day experience the thrill of climbing the statue. "Reopening the statue can mean only one thing: reopening all of it."

Charlie DeLeo, Keeper of the Flame

Charlie DeLeo is a volunteer who works inside the Statue of Liberty. He has been on the job for more than 30 years. DeLeo has made about 2,500 trips to the top of the statue's flame. He goes up to the top of her torch every month. There, he replaces burned-out lights and removes bird droppings.

Courtesy of Charlie DeLeo

153

Compare/Contrast Writing Frame

Use the Writing Frame below to orally summarize "Symbols of Our Country."

The symbols of our country are **similar** but also **different**. The

bald eagle is **like** the American flag in that _____

_____ .

But the bald eagle is _____ .

Unlike the bald eagle, the flag _____ .

Like the eagle and the flag, the Statue of Liberty _____

_____ .

The eagle and the Statue of Liberty **both** _____

_____ .

The Declaration of Independence is **different** from the eagle, the

flag, and the Statue of Liberty because _____ .

But like the other symbols, the Declaration of Independence _____

_____ .

Use the frame to write the summary on another sheet of paper. Be sure to include the **bold** signal words. Keep this as a model of this Text Structure.

Critical Thinking

1 Freedom from control by someone else is

called _____.

   A. strength

   B. liberty

   C. landmark

2 Point out the text in "Open Liberty!" that explains what the Statue of Liberty came to symbolize.

3 Find the paragraph about Charlie DeLeo. Why might he be called Keeper of the Flame?

4 Discuss with a small group the photograph of the Great Seal of California on page 151. Describe this seal. What does the word *Eureka* remind people of?

A photograph is a picture taken with a camera.

Digital Learning

For a list of links and activities that relate to this History/Social Science standard, visit the California Treasures Web site at www.macmillanmh.com to access the Content Reader resources. Have children visit the Field Trip "Washington, D.C."

PARTS OF OUR GOVERNMENT

The Constitution divides the United States government into three parts, or branches. The **legislative** branch is the Congress. It writes our laws. The **executive** branch makes sure the laws are followed. The President of the United States leads the executive branch. The third branch is the **judicial** branch, or our courts. They decide what the laws mean and if they follow the Constitution.

The legislative branch of California's state government is made up of the state assembly and the state senate. They make laws.

The head of a state's executive branch is the **governor**. The judicial branch reviews state laws to see if they are fair.

Local government makes the decisions that affect just a town or a city. There is often a **city council**, which is the legislative branch. It makes the laws. The **mayor** is the head of the city council. Citizens of the area vote for the mayor and the city council members.

◄ The California State Seal is a symbol of its government.

Legislative branch: Congress makes laws for our country. ▼

California, Native American Governments, and the United States

Like every state, California sends lawmakers to Congress and pays taxes to the federal, or national, government.

And like every other state, California sends representatives to Congress to represent the state. Congress has two parts, or houses. The Senate has 100 members, two for each state. The House of Representatives has 435 members. States with more people get to have more representatives.

Native Americans are citizens of the United States. However, they are also citizens of their tribes. Many tribes have their own governments. They elect their own leaders and make their own laws, but they also follow local, state, and national laws.

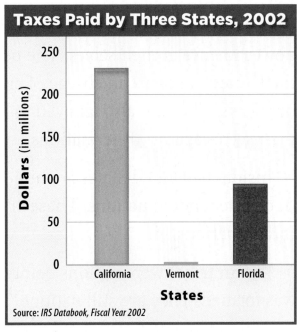

Taxes Paid by Three States, 2002

Source: *IRS Databook, Fiscal Year 2002*

▲ This graph compares California's share of taxes to that of two other states.

Tribal leaders and local leaders work together to solve problems. ▼

American Indian Nations

American Indian groups have their own nations within the United States.

The U.S. Capitol

The United States is a free, independent country—a nation. Its people have the power to govern themselves. The people of the United States are in charge of creating their own laws. They are also allowed to defend themselves against other nations.

Inside the United States are hundreds of other free, independent nations. These are American Indian nations.

Indian tribes were nations before the United States was formed. They are still nations. The Constitution of the United States says that Indian nations and the United States should deal with each other nation to nation.

Chippewa-Cree powwow at the Rocky Boy Reservation in Montana ▼

Marilyn Angel Wynn/Nativestock

The United States, though, doesn't have to deal with every group of Indians that calls itself a nation. Which groups are accepted as nations? There is a long, complicated process to decide. It can take years for the United States to decide that a group of Indians should be accepted as a nation.

To be accepted as a nation, the group of Indians must be able to show that it has been around since before the United States started. It may also have to show that the group has signed treaties that were accepted by the United States government.

Once a group of Indians is accepted as a sovereign, or self-governing, nation, it gains many important rights. These include:

- The right to create its own government

- The right to decide who is a part of its sovereign nation

- The right to manage relations among its members

- The right to decide who inherits what

- The right to tax members and nonmembers doing business with members

- The right to use and give out or sell land

- The right to make laws

American Indian nations have many rights. Still, there are limits. For example, Indian nations cannot put a non-Indian in jail. —*Lisa Jo Rudy*

Bettmann/Corbis

▲ Treaty-signing between the U.S. government and the Sioux in Wyoming, 1868

Marilyn Angel Wynn/Nativestock/Corbis

Flags of two nations: American and Santa Ynez Band of Chumash Indians ▶

Victoria Arocho/AP Photo

Narragansett Indian Tribal Police, Rhode Island ▶

Cause/Effect Writing Frame

Use the Writing Frame below to orally summarize "Parts of Our Government."

One **result** of the U.S. Constitution is that the United States

government is _____ .

Since the job of the executive branch is to make sure laws

are followed, the President of the United States _____

_____ .

Because the judicial branch includes our court system, _____

_____ .

A legislative branch writes laws. **Therefore**, California's _____

_____ .

The judicial branch includes the courts. This means that the

California judicial branch _____ .

Since local governments make the decisions that affect just a

town or city, _____ .

Use the frame to write the summary on another sheet of paper.
Be sure to include the **bold** signal words. Keep this as a model
for writing a summary of this Text Structure.

Critical Thinking

1 The head of the state's executive branch is the _____.

   A. mayor

   B. president

   C. govenor

2 Find the paragraph in "American Indian Nations" that describes what the Constitution of the United States says about Indian nations and the United States.

3 Reread in "American Indian Nations" the list of rights for a group of Indians accepted as a sovereign nation. Which rights seem the most important to you? Why?

4 Point out the bar graph on page 157. What information does this graph give?

> A bar graph is a drawing with bars whose lengths represent amounts.

Digital Learning

For a list of links and activities that relate to this History/Social Science standard, visit the California Treasures Web site at www.macmillanmh.com to access the Content Reader resources. Have children view the video "Many Communities, One Nation."

FIGHTERS FOR FREEDOM

We remember Anne Hutchinson as an American who stood up for freedom of religion. Freedom of religion is the right to practice any religion you choose or no religion at all. Anne was born in England and came to North America with her family in 1634. Her father taught her to think for herself and to speak her mind.

Anne was deeply religious. She began to meet with people in her home and talk about religion. Her ideas were different from what the ministers of her community taught. They had Anne arrested and put on trial for this. The court ordered Anne to leave the community. She left, but she never gave up her ideas or her right to think for herself.

Anne Hutchinson bravely fought for the right to believe in her own ideas. ▶

◀ Thomas Jefferson wrote most of the Declaration of Independence.

Benjamin Franklin fought for freedom and democracy. ▶

We remember Thomas Jefferson and Benjamin Franklin as Americans who helped our country gain independence from Great Britain. They were two of the men chosen in 1776 to write the Declaration of Independence. This document told Great Britain why Americans wanted to be free. Publishing the Declaration of Independence was the beginning of a long war with Britain.

Jefferson wrote that "all men are created equal." At that time, however, **slavery** was legal in the colonies. Slavery is the practice of keeping people against their wills and forcing them to work. In 1789, after our country won its freedom, Franklin asked Congress to end slavery, but Congress refused.

Thomas Jefferson

Thomas Jefferson had a lot of jobs.

The Granger Collection, New York

Thomas Jefferson was a busy man. He wrote the Declaration of Independence. He was President of the United States. He was also a farmer, a writer, and an inventor. He had many ideas that sounded wonderful. Sometimes he followed through on his ideas. Sometimes he didn't.

Thomas Jefferson (left) and others working on the Declaration of Independence ▼

Thomas Jefferson was born in 1743 to wealthy parents. He grew up on a plantation in Virginia. Jefferson trained to be a lawyer, but became a politician.

In 1776, Jefferson was in Philadelphia. He was one of Virginia's representatives to Congress. He wrote most of the Declaration of Independence and argued in favor of a revolution against the British.

The Granger Collection, New York

Monticello

In 1781 the American Revolution was still going on. The British had invaded Virginia. Even so, Jefferson said he was ready to quit politics. He thought it was time to go home. As it turned out, he didn't go home. He still had plenty of work to do.

Jefferson was elected governor of Virginia in 1779. In 1785 he became an ambassador to France. He became Vice President of the United States in 1796. He became President in 1800.

Jefferson said he didn't like big government. But with one stroke of his pen he made the Louisiana Purchase. Buying that land doubled the size of the United States. The Louisiana Purchase was as big as the rest of the United States.

Jefferson said he didn't like the idea of a permanent army. But it was Jefferson who created the U.S. Marines.

Jefferson wrote in the Declaration of Independence that all men are created equal. Jefferson, though, owned slaves. Nonetheless, as President, he signed a bill abolishing the slave trade.

After his second term as President, Jefferson went home to Virginia. There, in his home called Monticello, he designed the University of Virginia. He also wrote, invented new tools, and relaxed. —*Lisa Jo Rudy*

▼ Jefferson's plan for the University of Virginia

Compare/Contrast Writing Frame

Use the Writing Frame below to orally summarize "Fighters for Freedom."

Anne Hutchinson was an American who met with people to talk

about religion. **However**, her ideas _____

_____ .

Because her ideas were **in contrast** to other peoples' ideas, she was

_____ .

Thomas Jefferson **as well as** Benjamin Franklin were _____

_____ .

Both of these men were chosen _____ .

This document _____ .

Jefferson wrote that "all men are created equal." **However**,

slavery _____ .

In 1789, Benjamin Franklin asked Congress to end slavery, **but**

_____ .

Use the frame to write the summary on another sheet of paper.
Be sure to include the **bold** signal words. Keep this as a model
of this Text Structure.

Critical Thinking

1   The practice of keeping people and forcing them to work is called _____.

    A. independence

    B. bravery

    C. slavery

2   Reread the sentences in "Thomas Jefferson" about Thomas Jefferson's jobs. Name two of these jobs.

3   When did Thomas Jefferson become President of the United States? Point to the sentence in "Thomas Jefferson" that states this.

4   Compare and contrast the pictures and the captions of Anne Hutchinson, Thomas Jefferson and Benjamin Franklin, on pages 162 and 163.

A caption is a title or an explanation of a photograph.

Digital Learning

For a list of links and activities that relate to this History/Social Science standard, visit the California Treasures Web site at www.macmillanmh.com to access the Content Reader resources. Have children view the video "Many Communities, One Nation."

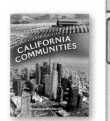

FREEDOM FOR ALL

We remember Harriet Tubman and Frederick Douglass as people who fought to free enslaved Africans. Harriet Tubman was born into slavery in the South. She escaped to the North, where she became free. For many years after her escape, Harriet Tubman risked her life leading other enslaved people to freedom. The routes she followed and the system of stopping places where people could hide were known as the **Underground Railroad**.

Frederick Douglass was also born into slavery and escaped to the North. There he started a newspaper. He used it to speak out against slavery. He also traveled and gave speeches. Later he served as an adviser to President Abraham Lincoln, who helped end slavery in the United States.

▲ Harriet Tubman fought to free enslaved people.

◄ Frederick Douglass also fought to free enslaved people.

We remember Dr. Martin Luther King, Jr., as a man who fought for freedom and fairness. He spoke out against **segregation**. Segregation is the separation of people by race or skin color. At one time African Americans could not eat in all of the same restaurants or go to all of the same schools as whites. King asked government leaders to change this. He led protests and marches, but he refused to use violence to meet his goals.

▲ Dr. Martin Luther King, Jr., won the Nobel Peace Prize in 1964.

We remember Elizabeth Cady Stanton and Susan B. Anthony as women who worked for more than 50 years to gain rights for women in the United States. In 1851 women had few rights. In most places they could not vote or own land. Elizabeth Cady Stanton and Susan B. Anthony wrote books, held meetings, made speeches, and talked to Congress about this. They are remembered for their struggles.

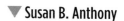

▼ Susan B. Anthony

◄ Elizabeth Cady Stanton

Abraham Lincoln and Frederick Douglass

A PRESIDENT AND A FORMER SLAVE FORMED A LASTING FRIENDSHIP.

Abraham Lincoln was President of the United States. Frederick Douglass was once a slave. What could these two men possibly have in common?

The Granger Collection, New York

The Granger Collection, New York

Both Lincoln and Douglass came from poor homes. Both men were big and tall. Both struggled to get the chance to learn to read and write. Both rose from poverty to become important. Both were wonderful writers and speakers. Both cared deeply about freeing slaves.

At first, Frederick Douglass didn't like Lincoln. Lincoln said he wanted to free the slaves, but Douglass thought he was taking too long to do it.

Douglass wanted an immediate end to slavery. He also wanted equal rights for men and women. He wanted black men to be part of the U. S. army. He even wanted everyone to be paid the same amount of money. These ideas upset many people, but Douglass felt that he was right.

Lincoln believed in most of the same ideals. Lincoln, though, wanted to move more slowly. Douglass became frustrated.

Then, on New Year's Day, 1863, Lincoln issued a statement. That statement, called the "Emancipation Proclamation," said that all men should be free. Soon Lincoln announced the end of slavery. He also announced that black men would be included in the U. S. army.

Bettmann/Corbis

▲ Lincoln reads the draft of the Emancipation Proclamation to his cabinet.

Douglass was thrilled. Soon the two men became friends. Douglass met with Lincoln at the White House.

When Lincoln was elected President for the second time, Frederick Douglass came to the inauguration. After Lincoln was sworn in, there was a big party. Policemen outside the White House tried to stop Douglass from coming in. They said that no black men were invited. Then Douglass sent word to Lincoln. Right away, word came to let Douglass in.

"Here comes my friend," Lincoln said, and took Douglass by the hand. "I am glad to see you. I saw you in the crowd today, listening to my inaugural address." He asked Douglass how he liked it, adding, "There is no man in the country whose opinion I value more than yours." —*Lisa Jo Rudy*

The Granger Collection, New York

▲ President Lincoln greets guests at a reception after his second inauguration.

Compare/Contrast Writing Frame

Use the Writing Frame below to orally summarize "Freedom for All."

Both Harriet Tubman and Fredrick Douglass _____

_____ .

Unlike Frederick Douglass, Harriet Tubman _____

_____ .

Like Harriet Tubman, Frederick Douglass _____

_____ .

Unlike Harriet Tubman, Frederick Douglass _____

_____ .

Douglass **also** _____ .

Like Harriet Tubman and Frederick Douglass, Dr. Martin Luther

King, Jr., _____ .

On the other hand, Elizabeth Cady Stanton and Susan B.

Anthony _____ .

Use the frame to write the summary on another sheet of paper.
Be sure to include the **bold** signal words. Keep it as a model of
this Text Structure.

Critical Thinking

1. The routes and stopping places where enslaved people traveling for freedom could hide were called the _____.

   A. Congress

   B. Underground Railroad

   C. United States

2. Find the sentences in "Abraham Lincoln and Frederick Douglass" that tell how Lincoln and Douglass were alike.

3. Point out the text in "Abraham Lincoln and Frederick Douglass" that tells what the Emancipation Proclamation said.

4. Identify the photographs of Harriet Tubman, Frederick Douglass, and Martin Luther King, Jr. on pages 168 and 169.

A photograph is a picture taken with a camera.

Digital Learning

For a list of links and activities that relate to this History/Social Science standard, visit the California Treasures Web site at www.macmillanmh.com to access the Content Reader resources. Have children read the biography "Susan B. Anthony."

FARMING IN CALIFORNIA

In California many people earn money from agriculture. Agriculture is the business of growing crops or raising animals for food. More food is grown in California than in any other state. In the heart of California's farming region, there is rich soil, water, and hot, dry summers. These are important natural resources for farming. This area is the perfect place to grow grapes, cotton, tomatoes, and many other crops.

Farms need **human resources** to help them grow crops or raise animals. Human resources are people, including owners and workers, who work for a business. Cher Sue and Bor Yang Lor own a small farm near Fresno. Their 13 children all help out on the farm that grows vegetables. This family has a lot of human resources!

Bor Yang Lor (left) and her daughter (right) sell their vegetables in Aptos, California.

In the past, children were often important human resources on a farm. They had regular chores to do. Animals had to be given food and water. Children helped out in the house as well. Many farm children only went to school when they didn't have to help with planting or picking the crops.

Capital resources are also an important part of farming and other businesses. Capital resources are the tools and machines people use to produce goods. In the past many farmers used capital resources such as horse-drawn machines. Even after gas-powered tractors were invented, some farmers still used horse-drawn machines.

Today most farms in California use capital resources such as tractors and computers.

In addition, some people work in businesses that provide services for farmers. People in government, for example, help farmers learn what works best on farms in California climates. These people also help to solve other problems.

Tractors are capital resources.

Children helped process food, such as peaches.

Turning Corn into Gold

A different way to use corn makes a big difference to a lot of people.

Royalty Free/Corbis

Farmers in the United States grow a lot of corn. In the past, corn was used mostly for food for people and animals. A few years ago, though, all that changed.

Ethanol is a fuel made from corn. It can replace gas in cars. When gas burns, it causes pollution. When ethanol burns, it causes much less pollution. The U.S. government decided that corn should be used to make ethanol.

To encourage farmers to grow corn for ethanol, the government said it would pay more for ethanol corn than for food corn. This extra money is called a subsidy (SUB•sih•dee).

Some farmers, like Bill Couser of Iowa, are excited about the ethanol subsidy. Couser has started a business. His business produces corn for ethanol. Other farmers in Iowa bought shares in Couser's company. That means they, like Couser, make money when the company makes money. So far, Couser and the other farmers have made a good deal of money from ethanol corn.

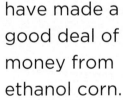

Matthew Staver/UPI/Landov

Corn-y gas causes less pollution. ▶

When farmers do well, the towns they live in do well, too. ▶

When the farmers make money, it doesn't end there. They spend their money. That means that stores and businesses near where the farmers live make more money. People all around the neighborhood get richer.

There's a problem, though. When Couser grows corn for ethanol, he grows less corn to use as food for animals. That makes this kind of corn more expensive. Farmers who raise those animals have to pay more for their food. And because the animal food is more expensive, products made from the animals are more expensive to buy. So beef, which comes from cows, costs more. So do pork, chicken, and even eggs.

Many people are feeling the pinch because of this change in the way we use corn. Popcorn costs more. The price of seed corn, which farmers buy to grow corn, is higher. That's tough enough for families in the United States. In poorer countries, it's even harder. If they can't afford corn, they may have nothing to eat. —*Lisa Jo Rudy*

▲ A high price for corn can make it hard for people in poorer countries.

◀ Expensive corn means expensive beef.

Problem/Solution Writing Frame

Use the Writing Frame below to orally summarize "Farming in California."

In California, many people earn money by _____.

In the heart of California, there are important natural resources for farming, but there is a **problem** if farms do not also have

_____.

To solve this problem, people such as Cher Sue and Bor Yang

Lor, who own a small farm, _____.

In the past, having enough human resources on a farm was also **a problem**. To solve this need, children often

_____.

Many farm children only went to school _____.

Today, capital resources such as _____ help people on farms in California **solve the problems** associated with producing goods.

Use the frame to write the summary on another sheet of paper. Be sure to include the **bold** signal words. Keep this as a model of this Text Structure.

Critical Thinking

1. The tools and machines people use to produce goods are
called _____.

    A. children

    B. capital resources

    C. human resources

2. Show a partner the sentence in "Turning Corn into Gold" that
gives the definition of ethanol.

3. Read aloud the text in "Turning Corn into Gold" that
describes what happens when farmers
make money.

4. Describe the photograph of the children with the
peaches on page 175. What does the caption tell
you about this photograph?

> A caption is a title
> or an explanation of
> a photograph.

Digital Learning

For a list of links and activities that relate to this History/Social
Science standard, visit the California Treasures Web site at
www.macmillanmh.com to access the Content Reader resources.
Have children view the video "Communities at Work."

MADE IN CALIFORNIA

Did you know that more products are made in California than in any other state in the country? Machines, clothes, toys, sports equipment, and many other things are made in California's **factories**. A factory is a place where products are made. Companies use natural resources, capital resources, and human resources. For example, a skateboard company needs wood, a natural resource, and machines to cut and shape the wood. The machines and the factory are capital resources. The people who design, cut, shape, and paint the skateboards are human resources.

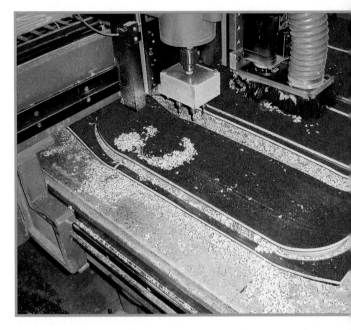

▲ Machines cut wood into skateboard shapes.

Businesses try to buy the natural resources they need for as low a price as possible. Sometimes that means buying natural resources from local businesses. Other times it means buying from businesses elsewhere in the United States or outside the country. A skateboard company in Santa Cruz, for example, might get its wood from Canada.

▲ People paint the skateboards.

Earning and Spending

People have jobs to earn **income**. Income is money received for working. The amount of income someone earns depends on the job he or she does. Right now, you work in school. By going to school and exploring different subjects, and by learning many skills, you are preparing to earn an income one day.

Many people use a budget to help them make smart spending choices. A budget is a plan for using money. A budget shows how much money is available and the ways that it will be spent.

Theo wants a new telescope so he can study the stars. His parents will look at their budget. It shows their total income for the month. It shows how much money is for expenses. An expense is money spent to buy something. Theo's parents will see if there is any money left to buy a telescope.

Family Budget

Income	Expenses
	Needs
Mom $1,756.00	Groceries $375.00
	Clothing $225.00
Dad $2,170.00	Rent $1,400.00
	College fund $150.00
	Wants
	Fun things $100.00

Money Counts

There are different ways to learn how to be smart about money.

Parents and children don't always agree about money. Parents want to teach their kids how to handle money wisely. Most kids have a long list of things they want to spend their money on. How can families find a balance between what parents and kids want?

Mowing lawns is one way to earn money.

"All parents hope they'll raise a money-savvy kid," says Peg Eddy. Her job is to help people use their money wisely. Eddy and most experts think the best way for kids to learn is by having a little money of their own. Some parents give money to their kids. Some parents say kids must earn their spending money.

Ryan is 17 years old and lives in Denver, Colorado. His parents say he should earn the money for things he wants. And he has done just that! Ryan has been mowing lawns since he was 8. Now he owns his own equipment. He has been able to save $7,800. He has also bought a dirt bike and a sound system.

Jayme Thorton/Getty Images

Smart kids know it's
important to save.

James Woodson/Getty Images

Save now, buy later!

Learn Now, Save Later

Money skills are important for
success. David Brady helps
children and young adults invest
their money. "Kids shouldn't be
consumed with money," he says.
He thinks they should learn the
basics of earning, saving, and
investing.

Talking About It

Many kids want to learn how
to handle their money. They know
that they may need it for college,
which is expensive.

Parents may think it's best to
teach kids what they shouldn't do.

But experts say a positive
message works better. For
example, parents can help kids
see that saving means thinking
about the future and waiting for
something that's important.

Teaching kids how to use
money doesn't have to mean
setting harsh rules. When
children are in charge of their
cash, they can learn to make
good rules for themselves.

Arthur Tilley/Taxi/Getty Images

Description Writing Frame

Use the Writing Frame below to orally summarize "Made in California."

Many interesting products are made in California.

For example, _____
are made in California factories.

Companies use resources that **include** _____

_____ .

For instance, a skateboard company _____

_____ .

The machines and the factory buildings are **examples** of _____

_____ .

The people who design, cut, shape, and paint the skateboards

are **examples of** _____ .

Businesses might buy the natural resources they need from

such places as _____ .

Use the frame to write the summary on another sheet of paper.
Be sure to include the **bold** signal words. Keep this as a model
of this Text Structure.

Critical Thinking

1. Money received from working is called _____.

   A. income

   B. expenses

   C. budget

2. Point out the sentences in "Money Counts" that tell how Ryan has earned money.

3. According to this article, how can children learn to make good rules about money for themselves? Find the text that supports your answer.

4. Discuss the chart on page 181 with a partner. What information does it give?

> A chart is a drawing that shows information in the form of a table, graph, or picture.

Digital Learning

For a list of links and activities that relate to this History/Social Science standard, visit the California Treasures Web site at www.macmillanmh.com to access the Content Reader resources. Have children read the biography "Cesar Chavez."

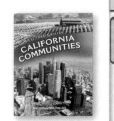

CALIFORNIA COMMUNITIES

Illustration Acknowledgements

54, 72, 90, 91(cr)(br): Tom Leonard. 78: Precision Graphics. 79: Vilma Ortiz-Dillon. 85, 91(b): Karen Minot. 132: Rich Stergulz

Photography Acknowledgements

All photos for Macmillan/McGraw-Hill except as noted below:

Cover: Alamy. 6: (tr) WoodyStock/Alamy; (br) Brian Pieters/Masterfile. 7: Alan Thornton/Stone/Getty Images. 12: Mauritius/age fotostock. 13: (cl) Lew Robertson/Food Pix/Jupiter Images; (br) Kevin Cruff/Taxi/Getty Images; (cr) Ian O'Leary/DK Images; (c) Madeline Polss/Envision. 18: (tr) C Squared Studios/Getty Images; (tr) V&A Images/Alamy; (tr) Stockbyte Silver/Alamy. 19: (b) Stocktrek/Brand X Pictures/Alamy; (cl) C Squared Studios/Getty Images. 24: Jim Cummins/Taxi/Getty Images. 25: (tr) David Keaton/CORBIS; (bl) Michael Keller/Index Stock. 30: (tr) Terry Oakley/Alamy; (b) David Muench/CORBIS. 31: (tl) David Fischer/Photodisc Red/Getty Images; (tr) Lisa Barber/Photonica/Getty Images. 36–37: DK Images (Dorling Kindersley Ltd.) Picture Library. 42: (tr) John Cancalosi/naturepl.com; (br) Richard Du Toit/naturepl.com. 43: (tr) Frank and Joyce Burek/PhotoDisc/Getty Images; (br) Owen Newman/naturepl.com. 48: (tr) Jay Syverson/CORBIS; (b) Danita Delimont/Alamy. 49: (cr) Paul Souders/The Image Bank/Getty Images; (br) Robert Harding Picture Library Ltd./Alamy. 60: (b) Ambient Images/Alamy. 61: Tom and Pat Leeson/Photo Researchers, Inc. 66: WorldFoto/Alamy. 67: (c) Steve Bloom Images/Alamy; (bl) Rod Patterson/ABPL/Animals Animals. 72: Peter Arnold, Inc./Alamy. 79: Comstock Images/Alamy. 96: (tr) Thomas Hallstein/Outsight Photography; (b) Bill Ross/CORBIS. 102: Robert Holmes/CORBIS. 103: Courtesy of The Department of Water and Power. 109: (br) A.W.Ericson/National Museum of the American Indian; (tcr) Denver Art Museum Collection: gift of Mrs. D. Bromfield. 114: American Museum of Natural History; (bl) Tim Street-Porter/Botanica. 115: California Academy of Science. 120: (cl) Terry W. Eggers/CORBIS; (br) San Diego Historical Society Davis Collection. 121: (tr) National Museum of the American Indian/Smithsonian Institution; (br) Edward H. Davis/The Constance DuBois Collection, San Diego Museum of Man. 126: Library of Congress. 127: (tr) Phoebe A. Hearst Museum of Anthropology; (b) Ed Kashi/CORBIS. 133: (tr) Jeff Gritchen; (b) Courtesy of the Choys; (cr) Courtesy of the Choys. 138: (b) courtesy of www.historichwy49.com; (tr) Courtesy of the Bancroft Library, University of California, Berkeley. 144: (b) Photo Edit; (tc) Joseph Sohm/ChromoSohm Inc./CORBIS; (cr) Photo Edit. 145: Bill Aron/PhotoEdit Inc. 150: Joseph Sohm/Visions of America/CORBIS. 151: (tl) One Mile Up Inc./Fotosearch; (cl) PhotoVault; (b) PhotoVault. 156: (b) Dennis Cook/AP WideWorld; (cl) One Mile Up, Inc./Fotosearch. 157: Ben Margot/AP Wideworld. 162: The Granger Collection. 163: (tl) The Granger Collection; (cr) Bettmann/CORBIS. 168: (tr) The Granger Collection; (bl) The Granger Collection. 169: (tr) Flip Schulke/CORBIS; (bl) The Granger Collection; (br) The Granger Collection. 174: (bl) (inset) George Wright. 175: (b) Compliments of Kings County Library; (cr) Renee Knoeber/AP-WideWorld. 180: (tr) (br) Rib Lake Plywood, Inc.